Red Riding Hood

A Pantomime

John Crocker

Lyrics and Music by
Eric Gilder

Samuel French–London
New York–Sydney–Toronto–Hollywood

The Vocal Score for this pantomime is available from Samuel French Ltd

Please note our NEW ADDRESS:

Samuel French Ltd
52 Fitzroy Street London W1P 6JR
Tel: 01 - 387 9373

CHARACTERS

RED RIDING HOOD.	
BO PEEP	Her Shepherdess.
DAME TROT	Her Grandmother.
SIR FALSE HOOD	The Squire.
HARDY HOOD)	
FOOLHARDY HOOD)	His sons.
BAA)	
BAA-BAA)	The Sheep.
PRINCE FLORIZEL	
POPPET	His Page.
THE DOWAGER FAIRY DUTIFUL	
DEMON SHEERSPITE	
LUPE	The Wolf.

CHORUS as Rustics, Goblins, Fairies, Beauticians, etc.

SYNOPSIS OF SCENES

ACT ONE

ACT TWO

SCENE 6   THE VILLAGE BEAUTY PARLOUR.

SCENE 7   OUTSIDE THE BEAUTY PARLOUR.

SCENE 8   THE SQUIRE'S BANQUET.

SCENE 9   IN THE WOODS.

SCENE 10   DAME TROT'S COTTAGE.

SCENE 11   WOLF CUBS.

SCENE 12   THE GRAND WEDDING RECEPTION.

Running time: Approximately two hours, thirty-five minutes, excluding interval.

PRODUCTION NOTE

Pantomime, as we know it today, is a form of entertainment all on its own, derived from a number of different sources - the commedia dell'arte (and all that that derived from), the ballet, the opera, the music hall and the realms of folk-lore and fairy tale. And elements of all of these are still to be found in it. This strange mixture has created a splendid topsy-turvy world where men are women, women are men, where the present is embraced within the past, where people are hit but not hurt, where authority is constantly flouted, where fun is poked at everything including pantomime itself at times, and, above all, where magic abounds and dreams invariably come true. In other words, it is - or should be - fun. Fun to do and fun to watch and the sense of enjoyment which can be conveyed by a cast is very important to the enjoyment of the audience.

Pantomime can be very simply staged if resources are limited. Basically a tab surround at the back, tab legs at the sides and a set of traverse tabs for the frontcloth scenes, together with the simplest of small cut-out pieces to suggest the various locales - or even just placards with this information written on them - will suffice. Conversely, there is no limit to the extent to which more lavish facilities can be employed. (I realise that Scene Five in the Haunted House is an exception to my suggestions above for very simple staging; as written much of it relies on scenic resources. Therefore, in cases where these are very limited, I am willing to allow producers to modify the scene to suit such limitations).

The directions I have given in the text adopt a middle course and are based on a permanent setting of a cyclorama skycloth at the back, a few feet in front of which is a rostrum about two feet high, running the width of the stage. About two thirds of the depth downstage is a false proscenium, immediately behind which are the lines for a set of traverse tabs. Below the false proscenium are arched entrances left and right, with possibly one foot reveals to the proscenium. A border will be necessary at some point between the false proscenium and the cyclorama to mask lighting battens and the top of the cyclorama. Lastly, there is a set of steps leading from the front of the stage into the auditorium, which I have referred to as the catwalk. I have imagined it to be set stage left, but it is unimportant whether it is left or right.

Into this permanent setting are placed various wings left and right; I have catered for one a side set on a level with the border, but a greater depth of stage may require two a side for masking purposes. Cut-out ground-rows set on the back of the rostrum complete the full sets. On smaller stages these cut-outs seen against the cyclorama give a better impression of depth than backcloths. The frontcloth fly lines come in behind the traverse tabs. Cloths can, of course, be tumbled or rolled if flying space is limited. It is a good tip always to bring in the traverse tabs when a cloth has to be lowered, then if any hitch occurs the lights can still come up and the actors get on with the scene. Similarly, I have indicated where the traverse tabs should be closed in frontcloth scenes so that there is plenty of time for the cloth to be flown before the end of the scene. The quick flow of one scene into the next is important if a smooth running production is to be achieved.

Sometimes the action escapes from the stage into the audience. Where this happens I have assumed an auditorium with aisles running the length of each side and transverse aisles at the front and about half way along its length. I have also assumed exits on each side and at the back of the auditorium, joined by passages out of sight of the audience, with a pass door from the stage into such a passage. These sequences will obviously have to be re-arranged to suit the auditorium used.

The settings and costumes should preferably be in clear bright colours to give a story book effect. It is probably best to try to have one overall period, but which period is immaterial. Also, of course, deliberate anachronisms should be introduced into some settings and some of the comics costumes. Animal skins can be hired from Theatre-Zoo, 28 New Row, W.C.2

I would suggest that Lupe's face is not obscured by a mask or a good deal of his comedy will be lost. The tree costumes for Hardy and Foolhardy in Scenes Three and Four can be made on tubular frames of chicken wire, covered with painted canvas. The frames should go from the top of their heads to their feet - with holes for their arms and faces - and widen out from the waist down to allow them some freedom of movement. A gap should be left at the back of each frame for them to get in and out, which is covered in wear by extending the canvas on either side to form an overlapping poppered join. The "boughs" should be separate sleeves of painted canvas with twig-like attached gloves.

Pantomime requires many props and often they will have to be home made. Instructions are given in the prop plot about any of the more awkward seeming ones. Props should be much larger than reality. It is wise for the property master to examine carefully the practical use to which a prop is to be put - it is very painful to be hit with a Giant's club of solid wood, one of material filled with foam plastic is far gentler!

I have not attempted to give a lighting plot as this entirely depends on the equipment available, but, generally speaking, most pantomime lighting needs to be full up, warm and bright. Pinks and ambers are best for this, but a circuit of blues in the cyclorama battens will help nightfall and dawn rising effects.

Follow spots are a great help for this kind of show, but not essential. But, if they are available, it is often effective in romantic numbers to fade out the stage lighting and hold the principals in the follow spots, quickly fading up on the last few bars as this frequently helps to increase the applause They can also be used for the Fairy and Demon to give them greater freedom of movement than with fixed front of house or spot-bar spots.

Flash boxes, with the necessary colour and flash powders, can be obtained from the usual stage electrical suppliers.

The music has been specially composed so that it is easy for the less musically accomplished to master, but it is also scored in parts for the more ambitious. If an orchestra is available well and good, but a single piano will suffice. It is an advantage, however, if there can be a drummer as well. Not only because a rhythm accompaniment enhances the numbers, but also because for some reason never yet fully fathomed slapstick hits and falls are always twice as funny if they coincide with a well timed bonk on a drum, wood-block or whatever is found to make the noise best suited to the action. A drummer can also cope with the various "whizzes" and "tings" noted in the directions, though if necessary they can, of course, be done off stage. A special type of whistle can be got for the "whizz" and the "ting" requires a triangle.

Pantomime demands a particular style of playing and production. The acting must be larger than life, but still sincere, with a good deal of sparkle and attack. Much of it must be projected directly at the audience, since one of pantomime's great advantages is that it deliberately breaks down the "fourth wall". The actors can literally and metaphorically shake hands with their audience who become almost another member of the cast- indeed, their active participation from time to time is essential. Word of warning on this, though - the actors must always remain in control; for instance, if a Demon or villain encourages hissing he must make sure it is never to such an extent that he can no longer be heard. The producer should see that the story line is clearly brought out and treated with respect. There is always room for local gags and topical quips in pantomime, but they should not be overdone. Most important of all, the comedy, as any comedy, must never appear to be conscious of its own funniness.

Characterization should be very clear and definite. I prefer the traditional use of a man to play the Dame and a girl to play the Principal Boy. In the case of the Dame, anyway, there is a sound argument for this - audiences will laugh more readily at a man impersonating a woman involved in the mock cruelties of slapstick than at a real woman. For this reason an actor playing a Dame should never quite let us forget he is a man, while giving a sincere character performance of a woman; further, he can be as feminine as he likes, but never effeminate. Dame Trot is a kindly, humorous and high spirited old lady, not at all abashed by the deficiences of her memory, or by anything else for that matter. She takes life as it comes and finds it comes very pleasant.

A Principal Boy also requires a character performance, but, of course, with the implications reversed! An occasional slap of the thigh is not sufficient. Prince Florizel could be thought of as a charming light comedian. He much enjoys his impersonation of a woodcutter not only becuase it frees him from the formal limitations of Princehood, but, more importantly, from the apalling shyness with which he is cursed. In spite of his high position he is without presumption and shows genuine humility in his wooing of Red Riding Hood.

Principal Girls can be a bore, but only if they are presented as mere pretty symbols of feminine sweetness. Red Riding Hood should be played with a lively sense of fun. She is very gay and fond of laughter and is not even above laughing at the man she loves - but she does love him and, what is more, intends to get him.

In contrast to Red Riding Hood's light heartedness Bo Peep is a worrier. She is also hopeless as a shepherdess, of which she is well aware since she is very conscientious. At the back of her mind is a fatalistic expectancy of failure, but nevertheless she tries to keep up a brave front.

Her charges, Baa and Baa-Baa, are obviously very tame sheep since they evince none of the timorousness associated with their breed. Indeed, mischieviousness is their chief characteristic, but they are never malicious - they plague Lupe for fun, nothing else. Baa-Baa is very much the leader and Baa the willing follower.

There is no trace of vindictiveness in Lupe, the wolf. His initial pursuit of people as possible meals is only an expression of his natural appetite. When this is taken from him he is easily made the victim of the intrigues of others. In short, he is a lone wolf who would much prefer to be left alone.

Poppet is very perky and shrewd. There can be a hint of cheekiness in his relationship with his master, but he is still a devoted and loyal servant. He is also highly resourceful and equal to most of the situations in which he finds himself.

Sir False Hood, the Squire, is a villain who relishes his villainy for its own sake, which is just as well since his schemes never turn out as he plans. He should be played with great gusto and it is important to remember that much of the story revolves round his machinations. In these he can hardly be said to be helped by his sons, Hardy and Foolhardy. Though they are willing enough to please him, somehow their efforts on his behalf always miscarry. They have very simple minds so it never occurs to them that there might be anything wrong in their father's intentions.

The Fairy Dutiful is an august immortal with abundant self-confidence. In fact, she is of that type for whom everything always goes right simply because she is so supremely and serenely sure it will. As she states, Demon Sheerspite is hardly worth her mettle. But he takes himself very seriously and tries hard to prove a creditable representative of evil, despite the ridicule his impediment bring him.

I have made provision for six members of the Chorus, but naturally the number used will depend on how many are available.

John Crocker

MUSIC 1.   OVERTURE

ACT ONE

Scene One - RED RIDING HOOD'S FARMYARD

(Full set. Ground-row cut-out at back of rostrum representing farm
scene. Steps down in C. of rostrum. Farmhouse piece set obliquely
L, with practical door, with two hay sheaves leaning against it. Barn
wing with practical door R. Long wooden rake R. Little flower bed in
front of R. proscenium arch, which is set throughout the pantomime.
It can of course be placed in front of L. proscenium arch if it is more
convenient to work it there.

CHORUS discovered as rustic lads and lasses.

MUSIC 2.   "WHAT A LOVELY MORNING".)

CHORUS: Oh, what a lovely morning
                 When the harvest's nearing
                 And the sheep need shearing.
         Oh, what a lovely morning
                 When the hay needs tedding
                 And the muck wants spreading.
         We leap out of bed before the dawning.
         We never complain - we just like yawning.
         Oh - (yawn) - what a lovely morning
                 To be working, working, working on a farm.

MUSIC 3

BO PEEP: (off L) Baa! Baa-Baa!

1ST CHORUS: Here comes Bo Peep. It sounds as if she's lost her sheep
     again.

2ND CHORUS: But of course, she'll pretend she hasn't.

BO PEEP: (entering L) Baa! Baa-Baa! B - Oh, hullo. (Starts to go
     again.)

3RD CHORUS: Looking for something, Bo Peep?

BO PEEP: (returning) What me? Looking? Oh no. That is, not
    exactly looking - just sort of - glancing. (Gives a little laugh which
    dies on her.) You havn't seen anything worth glancing for, have you?

4TH CHORUS: What sort of thing?

BO PEEP: Two things actually, about so high , (Indicates with hand.)
    and rather - rather -

5TH CHORUS: Woolly?

BO PEEP: Well, yes, I was going to say fluffy, but I suppose you could say woolly.

R. R. H. :   (off, in farmhouse L) Bo Peep! Bo Peep!

BO PEEP: Oh dear, here comes Red Riding Hood, and I've lost her woollies, I mean, her fluffies - I mean, oh dear and it's her birthday too.

6TH CHORUS: So it is.

(MUSIC 4.   Enter RED RIDING HOOD from farmhouse, L.)

CHORUS: Happy Birthday, Red Riding Hood.

BO PEEP: Yes, many happy returns of the day and - one or two other things.

R. R. H. :   How are you getting on with your sheep?

BO PEEP: Baa and Baa-Baa? Oh, very well, although - er - they have been a little distant with me today.

R. R. H. :   Ah. Perhaps that's why I thought I saw them wandering down to the village.

BO PEEP: To the village? Oh no - they might wander into the butcher's and - oh dear. (Running off R.) Sometimes I think I ought never to have been a shepherdess. Baa! Baa-Baa!

R. R. H. :   Poor Bo Peep, perhaps she's right. Still, I can't talk, I'm not much good as a farmer. All I seem to do is sell things to pay the royal rent. But I do wish the Squire wouldn't do his job as collector of the King's rents so efficiently. After all he is my cousin and yet because of him the sheep are about all I have left now that are worth selling. Still, I'm sure something will turn up soon.

1ST CHORUS: Yes, probably the Squire. It's royal rent day again.

R. R. H. :   Again? Oh dear. I'd better keep out of his way. I'll walk through the wood and visit granny.

2ND CHORUS: Mind you don't meet the wolf then.

R. R. H. :   I don't believe there is one. Sometimes I wish there was so that I could be rescued from him by a handsome stranger. I'm eighteen now. It's high time something exciting happened in my life. If I'm not careful I'll be nineteen and too old for excitement. I insist on adventure from now on.

MUSIC 5. "BEFORE I GROW TOO OLD".

Tell me of cities with lovely surprises:
Tell me the place where the great river rises;
   Tell me the tales that the old men told
   Before I grow too old.
I want the joy of the bright lights and dances,
I want the life of the greatest romances,
I want the days when the knights are bold
   Before I grow too old.
I want to ride
On the furthermost tide,
   And fly off to distant lands;
I want to dine with rarest of wine,
   And hold jewels in my hands.
Show me the West that the sun is forsaking,
Show me the East where the new day is making;
   I want to look for the crock of gold
   Before I grow too old.

I'm of an age
When the world is my stage,
   And I want to play my part.
I've made my goal
The prominent role
   That's written upon my heart.
Give me of love, and be free with your giving
Give me a logical reason for living
Give me the man I can have and hold
   Before I grow too old.

(Exit RED RIDING HOOD D. L.   Sound of horses hooves off R.)

3RD CHORUS: Red Riding Hood got away just in time.   Here's the Squire now.

4TH CHORUS: Yes, showing off as usual.   Pretending he's got a horse and all the while just banging coconut shells together.

5TH CHORUS: You mean he's doing his nut.

(Others laugh.)

SQUIRE: (off R) Whoa back there, my beauty!

(Hooves come to a stop in a flurry of whinnying and horse-like blowing from SQUIRE.)

6TH CHORUS: He is too. Well, we'd better do our nuts and pretend to work, then maybe he won't realise Red Riding Hood hasn't any money.

(MUSIC 6. They are grouped in two equal lines either side of stage. 6TH CHORUS gets sheaves and throws one to head of R. group, who pass it down their line, while 6TH CHORUS passes other sheaf up the line on her side. As the sheaves reach the other ends of each line they are thrown over simultaneously to the other group and again passed along and kept. During this the SQUIRE enters R, twirling his curly moustaches with one hand and hiding the coconut shells behind his back with the other. He strides in between the two groups so that the sheaves are flying just behind and in front of his head.)

CHORUS: Good morning, Sir False Hood.

SQUIRE: Good morning, yokels. Is your - (Dodging sheaves.) - what are you playing at with those things?

1ST CHORUS: Sorry, Squire, we're very busy haymaking.

(Both sheaves are thrown so that they hit him in the face.)

SQUIRE: Look out!

(CHORUS fall to brushing him down very vigorously.)

CHORUS:) Beg pardon. So sorry, Squire etc.
) (together)
SQUIRE:) All right, all right, that's enough.

2ND CHORUS: (knocking the coconut shells from his hand and picking them up) Oh dear, I think your horse has shed a couple of shoes, Squire.

(CHORUS laugh.)

SQUIRE: What? Oh, nonsense. That's the remains of my do-it-yourself Bounty bar. (Snatches them away and throws them off.) Is your mistress at home?

3RD CHORUS: What a pity, you've just missed her. She will be sorry.

4TH CHORUS: (picking up wooden rake from R) Excuse us, Squire, we've got some work to do in the yard. (Moving across SQUIRE and catching him with the end of rake nearly pulling him over.) Oh, sorry, Squire, I didn't mean to start it here.

SQUIRE: Start what here?

2ND CHORUS: Muck raking.

(CHORUS move off L, laughing.)

SQUIRE: Beastly buccolic boobies. I don't believe they've got any work to do, anyway. Surely I must have bled their mistress, my pretty little distant cousin, dry by now? I must force her to marry me somehow. Supposing that long lost will suddenly turns up? She'd learn that now she's eighteen she is the true heiress to the Hood fortunes and I should be penniless. But if I get her to marry me then whatever happens I'll still retain control of the money. Besides, my two poor motherless little lads need a woman's hand to guide them.

MUSIC 7.

HARDY,
FOOLHARDY: (off R) Papa! Papa!

SQUIRE: Ah, here come the little dears - blast them!

(HARDY HOOD and FOOLHARDY HOOD scoot on R. on a twosome two-way scooter, which has wheels and handlebars at each end. HARDY faces L. and FOOLHARDY R. and both are trying to steer with their heads down to the task so they do not see SQUIRE.)

FOOLHARDY: You're going the wrong way, Hardy.

HARDY: (making progress to the L) Kindly leave this to me, Foolhardy. He's this way.

SQUIRE: Boys, stop play - Oi! (Just dodges upstage out of scooters way in time and hastily moves R.)

FOOLHARDY: He's not, he's this way. (Propels it to R.)

SQUIRE: Look out! (Dodges upstage and to L.)

HARDY: (propelling scooter to L) No, this way!

(SQUIRE starts to run R.)

FOOLHARDY: (propelling it to R) This way!

SQUIRE: (running back to L) I suppose you know this is a one way street.

BOTH: (trying to scoot in their opposite directions so that scooter remains stationary.) THIS WAY!

FOOLHARDY: Ooh, we've got stuck.

HARDY: Got what?

FOOLHARDY: (stopping scooting and turning to speak) Stuck!

          (Scooter shoots forward to L, just as SQUIRE turns away in shrugging
          despair and HARDY buffets him in behind with his head and knocks him
          down.)

HARDY: Ah, papa.

SQUIRE: Yes, and look what you've done you - you fool, Hardy.

HARDY: You're getting confused, papa.   He's Foolhardy - I'm Hardy.

SQUIRE: I mean - oh, never mind.

HARDY: We were afraid we'd miss you, papa.

SQUIRE: Well, you didn't.   (Rises, rubbing bottom.)

HARDY: We've been looking for you, papa, to bring you this letter.
          We thought it looked important.   (Hands SQUIRE a very imposing looking
          letter sealed with a large red seal.)

SQUIRE: Hm, yes. (Opening it.)   Now then, lets see - Oh, I can't,
          I haven't got my glasses.   You have a butchers.   (Gives letter to HARDY.)

HARDY: I haven't got my glasses either, papa.

FOOLHARDY: I have! I have! (Puts on a large pair of glasses.)

S QUIRE: (taking the letter from HARDY and gives it to FOOLHARDY)
          All right, you read it.

FOOLHARDY: Oh, I can't do that.

SQUIRE: Why not?

FOOLHARDY: I can't read.

SQUIRE: Tcha! (Snatching letter away.)   That means none of us can
          read it.

HARDY: (taking letter) I can, papa.

SQUIRE: But you just said you hadn't got your glasses.

HARDY: I know.   But I don't use glasses for reading.

SQUIRE: (splutters furiously for a moment) Oh, get on and read it.

HARDY: Yes, papa. (Examining letter.) Ooh, fancy that. Well,
     I never.   Um. That's interesting. (Gives letter back.) I've read
     it, papa.

SQUIRE: Out loud, boy! Who's it from?

HARDY: The King.

SQUIRE: The King! Is it about his rents for the last twelve months?

HARDY: No, papa.

SQUIRE: That's a relief. What's he say, then?

HARDY: Er-hm. Sir False Hood, know ye by these presents -

FOOLHARDY: Has he sent presents? Oh, goody!

SQUIRE: No, he has not, it's just an expression. It means - er -
     Do read the letter, Hardy.

HARDY: Know ye by these presents that we send greetings to our
     faithful subject. Our son, Prince Florizel, is touring our Kingdom to
     make himself known to his future subjects and it is our wish that he
     includes a visit to yourself. Accordingly his Highness will arrive one
     week hence and we bid ye loyally to make him welcome. Hoping this
     finds ye as it leaves we, X. Rex, his mark.

FOOLHARDY: X. Rex? That's a funny name for a King.

SQUIRE: It's not his name. It's his trade mark. You lads nip home
     and tell them to prepare for the Prince's visit. I still want to see Red
     Riding Hood. It might help if I spruced myself up a bit. I'll pop to the
     barber's and have a quick shave. Well, don't just stand there - get
     going!

HARDY: Righto, papa. Come, Foolhardy, and let's go the right way
     this time.

FOOLHARDY: Yes, the right way.

     (Both mount scooter, HARDY facing L and FOOLHARDY R. HARDY
     propels it off L.)

SQUIRE: Hey, wait! You numskulls, that isn't the right way, Ah,
     well. (Moves to exit R. as they come charging back from L. with
     FOOLHARDY propelling it.)

FOOLHARDY: No, Hardy this is the right way. (His bent-down head biffs
     SQUIRE in rear and knocks him flat.)

Ooh. Let's go the wrong way. (He hurriedly turns to face
other way and they scoot off L. as SQUIRE rises and chases after them.)

SQUIRE: You barrenbonced bumblebrains! Come back! Come back, you
nit-headed ninnyhammers. Come back! (Exit D. L.)

(MUSIC 8. POPPET enters U. L. carrying two suitcases, one very large
in his L. hand and a tiny one in his R. with a royal crest on it.)

POPPET: Whew! I'm exhausted having to carry the Prince's luggage
and my own. And I'm sure he's got too much in his. (Holds up small
case, then puts both down and opens large case.) I only carry essentials
in mine. (Takes out a small portable chair and sits on it.) Well, here's
a fine thing. Not a soul in sight to welcome Prince Florizel. Still, I'm
always prepared for emergencies. (Takes out and displays a small red
carpet and puts it down. The succeeding articles are placed on it.)   I'd
better put the cheer record on for him too. (Takes out portable gramophone.
Oh no, I'm forgetting, he doesn't want to be welcomed. We're not officially
expected till next week. By the way, I hope you don't mind me chatting to
you like this. (Rises and moves D. C.) My name's Poppet. What's yours?
Eh? I couldn't quite catch. Try again, what's your name? No, no, don't
be shy and whisper - be bold and bellow - WHAT'S YOUR NAME? Um.
Funny sort of name that. I'm the Prince's page. It's quite a tiring job
in some ways. (Yawns.) In fact, I think I could do with a nap. (Takes
a bedding roll from case and spreads it on ground.) Not that I'm complaining
he's a very nice fellow the Prince. Funny thing though, he's terribly shy
with young women. Really. If a pretty young woman so much as flutters an
eyelash at him he's finished - can't say a word. (Gets into bedding roll.
Yawns.) You will pardon me if I have a little doze, won't you? Night-
night. (Lies down, then looks up again.) Tt-tt, I'm forgetting the lights.
(Takes out a board with a switch fitted to it.) Night-night again. (Clicks
switch. BLACKOUT. Pause. POPPET gives a snore and a whistle or
two.)

PRINCE: (off L.) Poppet! Poppet!

POPPET: (sleepily) Eh? What's that?

PRINCE: (off) Poppet!

POPPET: Cor, the Prince! Yes, sir, here, sir! (Bangs about in the
dark.) The switch, the switch, where's the switch? Oi, turn on the
lights while I find the switch.

(LIGHTS UP.)

Right, got it.

(BLACKOUT. The red carpet and all the things on it are whisked off
stage and POPPET throws bedding roll off. POPPET clicks the switch.
LIGHTS UP. POPPET is just shutting case.)

There, all packed and ready.   Just in time too, here he comes.

(MUSIC 9.   Enter the PRINCE U. L. and strides to C.)

PRINCE: Ah, Poppet, the coast is clear I take it.

POPPET: Yes, sir, you're quite safe, I haven't seen a single young
lady.

PRINCE: I didn't mean only them.   Have you seen anybody?

POPPET: No, sir.   But don't tell me your shyness is spreading to
everybody now?

PRINCE: No, this is rather a different matter we have to deal with.
But I've had an idea how to go about it, which might help to cure my
shyness too.

POPPET: Oh, good, sir.   What is it?

PRINCE: Woodcutters.

POPPET: Yes!   Eh?

PRINCE: Woodcutters.   We are.   Well, we will be.

POPPET: And that's going to help cure your shyness?

PRINCE: It might.   I mean, just not being myself for a while might
bring me out of myself and help me to forget myself when I am again.

POPPET: I'm sure you're right, sir.   But why woodcutters?

PRINCE: Because there's lots of woods round here, so nobody will
take much notice of us.   Look, I'll explain from the beginning.   Why do
you think we're here a week early?

POPPET: Er - your watch was fast?

PRINCE: No!   Because when we arrive officially next week we'll be the
guests of the Squire.   He's father's rent collector for the village but he
hasn't sent in any rents for about a year. Well, while we're under his roof
he won't give us much chance to find out what he's been up to, so -

POPPET: Woodcutters!   Very neat, sir.   The only thing is you don't
look like one.   I might pass muster, but - never mind.   Luckily I packed
your mod gear.   (Picks up PRINCE'S suitcase.)

PRINCE: My mod gear?

POPPET: Yes, your leather tunic and trunks.   You can change in this
     barn here.   (Puts PRINCE'S suitcase inside barn.)

PRINCE: Thank you, Poppet.   Oh, and Poppet, we'll need a couple of
     axes.

POPPET: Axes?   Ah, well it just so happens - (Opens own suitcase and
     takes out two axes.)

PRINCE: Well, I never!   What are you doing with these, Poppet?

POPPET: Oh, I'm always prepared for anything, sir - even a touch of
     the woodcutters.   (Exit into barn with own suitcase and the axes.)

PRINCE: Surprising fellow Poppet.   Well anyway, that's made a start
     on one of the tasks father gave me.   I'm not looking forward to the other
     though.   Finding a wife's rather a tall order for somebody who can't
     even speak to a girl.   And yet - I always know just what to say and just
     how to say it - until I can't.

          (MUSIC 10.   "SHOCKINGLY SHY" U.C. and L.C. tab.)

                    I'm the victim of a great affliction,
                    And I wish someone would tell me why.
                    The thing I have learn'd is where girls are concerned
                         I'm shockingly shy.

                    You would think that I could smile or wink
                    Each time a pretty lady passes by.
                    But every girl sees me go weak at the knees -
                         I'm shockingly shy.

                    I tell you I am truly terrified,
                    I don't know what or when or how:
                    A fact that easily is verified -

          (Looking off.)

                    'Cos I think a girl is coming along right now!   Wow!

          (Starts to back away then indicates the danger is past.)

                    Deep inside I've really tried and tried
                    And tried to look a person in the eye.
                    I rave and I rant, it's no good, I just can't!
                         I'm shockingly shy.

> I'm haltingly, hopelessly,
> Horribly, helplessly,
> Shatteringly, shockingly
> Shy.

(He goes off U.R. BLACKOUT. MUSIC 11. Sound of a very powerful motor car off L. (grams) and loud hooting. Two powerful car headlight beams sweep on from L. curving round and coming towards AUDIENCE. Car sounds as if it is braking to a screeching halt. LIGHTS UP and we see DAME TROT behind a car steering wheel fitted onto a cross bar which holds the car headlamps.)

DAME TROT: Hullo. Ooh, I seem to have forgotten the rest of my car. I wonder if that's because I've forgotten to pay for it? (Puts 'Car' off L.) I'm afraid my memory isn't all that good. Still, I am pleased to see you all. My name is - er - er - Wait a bit - it'll be marked inside my clothes. (Pulls at her neck band and cranes her neck round to read tab at back of collar.) Bri Nylon. No, that can't be right. I'll try the underwear department. (Starts to lift skirts.) What's this? I didn't come out wearing a bustle. (Finds shopping basket suspended from her waist over her behind.) So that's where my shopping got to. (Puts basket by farmhouse door and finds laundry mark inside leg of her red flannel knickers.) Ah, here we are, I'm - Double O Seven? James Bond? Seems unlikely. Ah, I know how I'll find out. (Moves over catwalk into AUDIENCE and speaks to one of them.) May I look at your programme? Thank you so much. Now then ... yes, I'm (Local Theatre personality.)

M.D.: You're not. You're Dame Trot.

DAME: Am I? (Looks at programme.) So I am. (Gives programme back, and moves back on stage.) Thank you so much and thank you Mr. - Er?

M.D.: (the M.D. gives his name)

DAME: (repeating it) Are you doing anything special here?

M.D.: Only playing music

DAME: Playing music? How interesting. I'm here to - to - (Finds red riding hood in basket.) to fight a bull? Oh no, no, no, no. (Crosses to lean against R. pros. arch.) Really, I must do something about this memory of mine. I find nibbling the leaf of a forget-me-not quite helpful. In fact, I planted a forget-me-not the other day so I could always have some leaves handy. The only trouble is, I've forgotten where.

(Forget-me-not flower with one leaf pops up from the little flower bed in front of R pros. arch.)

Well, what a coincidence! Now perhaps I can remember why I came here. (Pulls leaf off and takes a bite. Plant subsides.) Ah yes, to give this red riding hood to Red Riding Hood. You see I make her one every year for her birthday. This year she's (Takes another bite,) Eighteen? Goodness gracious wasn't there something special I had to tell her on her eighteenth birthday? (Nibbles thoughtfully at leaf.) Yes, her father was a descendant of - whatshisname? (Swallows last bit of leaf.) Oh, Robin Hood and that's why I've something important to tell Red Riding Hood, which is - which is - Oh dear, I've run out of leaf. Um, so's the forget-me-not. I'll have to wait till it grows another one. Still, it works very well, doesn't it? But what if I forget to remember my forget-me-not? I know, you can help me. Whenever I need a little assistance I shall say, "Reminder, please" and I want you to shout back "Forget-me-not". Let's try it. Reminder, please.

(AUDIENCE shout.)

Not bad, but my memory's a little hard of hearing sometimes so try shouting a bit louder. Ready? REMINDER, PLEASE.

(AUDIENCE shout.)

Oh, very good. In fact, it was so good it's almost made me forget what we're doing it for - REMINDER, PLEASE.

(AUDIENCE shout.)

Splendid, splendid. I'm so pleased with that I think I'll burst into song. Perhaps you could give me a little help there - er - er - Wilfrid.

M.D. :   Do you mean me?

DAME: Of course I do - William. You play some music and I'll forget the words. Er –one, er –two, er –four!

MUSIC 12. "TUM TI TUM".

When I was a little girl my Mother sang to me
A song that will for ever more live in my memory
The sound of that beloved voice, I seem to hear it yet;
The message of those lovely words I never will forget.
It - goes -
Tum ti tum ti tiddly tum and tum ti what's itsname.
And something something thingumybob and tra la la la la,
And tiddly-push and oo-ja-ma-flip and tumtifum ti tay -
    Oh, I'm sure you know the little song I mean!

Now Mother is an angel, and she's oh, so far away;
But if I'm good I hope I'll be an angel too some day;
Then when I get to Heaven I will see her face again,
And hear her sweet voice sing that unforgetable refrain.

It - goes -
Tum ti tum etc.

Oh, I'm sure you know the little song,
I know you know the little song,
    You're bound to know the little song I mean.

(She goes off D. L.   Enter RED RISING HOOD U. L.)

R. R. H. :   Well, that was a wasted journey.   Granny wasn't at home
and nothing in the least exciting happened - no wolf to be rescued from
and, anyway, no handsome stranger to rescue me.

(Enter FLORIZEL from barn now in leather tunic etc.)

PRINCE: Yes, this should do.   Oh, my axe.   (Goes back into barn.)

R. R. H. :   Ooh, there's one though.   (Running U. L. to look off.)   Oh
quick, where's the wolf?   (Sigh.)   Not there, of course.   Still, surely
I could be excused one little cry of help.

(PRINCE re-enters carrying axe.)

PRINCE: There, now I'm - (Sees RED RIDING HOOD and stops dead.)

R. R. H. :   Maybe even two.

PRINCE: Oh, dear, I - er - I - er - (Turns away in confusion and calls
urgently to barn in low voice.)   Poppet!   Poppet!

R. R. H. :   Oh, definitely two cries of help.   (Opens her mouth to give
them.)

PRINCE: Help!   Help!

R. R. H. :   (moving down)   You've taken the words right out of my mouth.

PRINCE: Poppet!

POPPET: (puts head out sees R. R. H.)   Woodcutters!   (Pushes PRINCE
to C and disappears.)

R. R. H. :   Woodcutters?

PRINCE: (beginning with great difficulty)   Yes, me.   I am.   A
woodcutter.   I'm a woodcutter.   That's it, I'm a woodcutter.   (Realises
he is managing to talk to her.)   I'm a woodcutter!   I'm a woodcutter!

R. R. H. :   I think I've gathered that now.   You're a woodcutter.

PRINCE: (laughing) I'm sorry, but, you see, you're practically the first woman I've ever spoken to.

R. R. H. :   Really? I'd no idea woodcutting was so lonely. I'm a farmer.

PRINCE: A farmer? I'd no idea farmers were so pretty. Oh, I'm sorry, now I've started, my tongue's running away with me.

R. R. H. :   That's all right, I rather like the way it's running. Could it run so far as to tell me your name?

PRINCE: Florizel. Oh. Perhaps it oughtn't to be, though.

R. R. H. :   Why not? It's a nice name. The same as the Prince.

PRINCE: Yes, exactly the same. I mean, I was named after him.

R. R. H. :   I was named after my red riding hood. At least, I wasn't really, but everybody calls me that because I always wear one. I have to, you see, my grandmother has such a bad memory that unless I do, she can't remember who I am. The Hood bit's right, but I should be Rosemary Rosalind not Red Riding. Still, at least the initials are the same. Granny makes them for me herself and brings me one each year for my birthday. (Sees DAME TROT'S basket by farmhouse door.) Ah, that's why she was out. Look. (Holds up red riding hood.)

PRINCE: You mean, it's your birthday today? May I wish you many happy returns?

R. R. H. :   Thank you.

PRINCE: I shall wish them to myself too.

R. R. H. :   Why, is it your birthday as well?

PRINCE: No, but I'd like many happy returns of meeting you.

MUSIC 13.   "HAPPY RETURNS".

                    Happy returns,
                    Let us have many happy returns
                         Of this magic meeting.
                    Moments like this,
                    Such unusual moments as this
                         Are worth repeating.
                    Though our words have blended,
                    Soon our moment's ended,
                         Off we must go to worlds away.
                    So with this song I sing you,
                    Out of my heart I bring you

Greeting -
Many returns of this happy day.
(Exit RED RIDING HOOD into farmhouse.)

PRINCE: Poppet! Poppet!

POPPET: (running on from barn) Sir?

PRINCE: Poppet, it's worked! I talked to her. I actually talked to
her. Isn't that wonderful?   (Slaps POPPET heartily on back in his
exuberance.)

POPPET: (tenderly rubbing shoulder-blade) Yes, wonderful, sir.

PRINCE: For the first time in my life I managed to talk to a girl.
Why, it's - it's marvellous.   (Slaps POPPET on back again.)

POPPET: (wincing with pain) Ooh! Marvellous. Still, we mustn't
forget the main idea's to see what we can find out about the Squire.

PRINCE: Quite right, Poppet. I'll go down to the village and start
rightaway. Oh, Poppet, I feel so - so - oh, I don't know what I feel!
(Gives POPPET a final thump and goes of L. happily while POPPET
stifles a cry of agony.)

POPPET: Well, I know what I feel - black and blue. I'd better put in
an extra pair of shoulder pads in case he talks to any more pretty girls.

BO PEEP: (off R) Baa! Baa-Baa!

POPPET: (looking off R) Aye-aye, my turn now. Let's see what a
little woodcutting does for me.

(Enter BO PEEP R.)

BO PEEP: Baa! Baa-Baa! (Looks around, sighing.)

POPPET: Excuse me, miss.

BO PEEP: (nods and smiles to him as she crosses to call off L, below
farmhouse.) Baa! Baa-Baa! Baa-Baa' Baa!

POPPET: Er - miss -

BO PEEP: (shrugs and crosses D.R to call off there, smiling and
nodding to POPPET as she does so) Baa-ah! Baa-Baa-ah!

POPPET: (moving to her) Do you speak English at all?

BO PEEP: Oh, yes, always. (Crosses him to call off D. L.) Baa!
Baa-Baa! Baa! I'm calling my sheep. I've sort of - mislaid them,
you see.

POPPET: (glancing off R.) Well, what about the couple coming down the road now - the black and the white one?

BO PEEP: (looking) Oh no - mine were the other way round, one white and one bl- (Realises what she is saying and takes on it.) It's them!

SHEEP: (off R.) Baa!

BO PEEP: You've found them! Oh, you darling! (Kisses and hugs him impetuously then breaks away.) Ooh, what am I thinking of?

POPPET: I don't know, but tell the sheep to go away and let me find 'em again!

SHEEP: Baa!

    (MUSIC 14. SHEEP enter and run to BO PEEP affectionately.)

BO PEEP: Oh, you naughty sheep, I'm so pleased to see you.

SHEEP: (the sheep rub their heads against her legs)

BO PEEP: But I'm very cross with you, too.

SHEEP: (the sheep hang their heads in mock shame, then give her a sidelong glance and emit a small pleading - "Baa.")

BO PEEP: Still, I'll forgive you this time. Now, introduce yourselves nicely. This is -

BAA: (pointing to herself with a hoof) Baa.

POPPET: Baa? Hm, original name for a sheep, that.

BAA: (Baa nods and drops a curtsey with her hind legs)

POPPET: Oops, I think your rear suspension's gone.

BO PEEP: It's all right, she's a ewe.

    (BAA rises.)

POPPET: A me?

BO PEEP: No, not a you you, a ewee ewe. You know, a sheep lady.

POPPET: Oh, I see. Beg pardon.

BO PEEP: And this is her brother.

BAA-BAA: (points to himself with a hoof) Baa-Baa.

POPPET: Ah, Baa-Baa black sheep, of course. How do you do?
(Takes the R leg BAA-BAA offers him and shakes it.)

BO PEEP: And now, off you go to your pen, like good little sheep.

(BAA-BAA shakes head mischieviously, BAA follows suit, and they lie
down, looking cheekily up at her. She regards them helplessly.)

BO PEEP: I do wish sheep weren't so wilful. It's Baa-Baa's fault.
He just leads his sister on.

POPPET: Ah, the black sheep of the family, eh? I know how to deal
with them, though. (POPPET gives a sharp bark and they jump up
immediately. He barks again and they snap to attention. POPPET
gives four barks and BAA right-dresses on BAA-BAA: two barks and
they turn L: two more and they quick march POPPET barking to the
rhythm of "left-right, left-right". At exit above farmhouse BAA-BAA
turns his head and throws up his back heels derisively. POPPET gives
an extra sharp bark and BAA-BAA scuttles off.)

POPPET: All right?

BO PEEP: Oh, splendid! Have you handled sheep before?

POPPET: No, we don't get any sheep at cour - I mean, in the woods.
I'm a woodcutter you see. And I suppose I ought to go and cut a few
woods down. Yes. (Plonks axe on shoulder with a rather too forcible
flourish.) Ouch!

BO PEEP: Ooh, does it hurt? Shall I kiss it better?

POPPET: Yes, please.

BO PEEP: (kisses his shoulder) All right?

POPPET: Not quite. The pain's sort of spreading - all up here.
(Indicates up neck and onto face.) It's very bad just there. (Points to
lips.)

BO PEEP: (almost kisses his lips) I don't think I know you well enough
to kiss you better there.

POPPET: Then let's get to know each other well enough.

BO PEEP: How?

MUSIC 15.   "GET TO KNOW YOU BETTER".

BOTH: Come about a half-inch nearer
                    So that I can see you somewhat clearer.
                      Try to come a little closer still
                        And then I'll get to know you better.
                    Turn your face in my direction
                    Till I see in detail your complexion
                        And my curiosity fulfil,
                        And then I'll get to know you better.
                    You appear just right for size,
                    With two most interesting eyes,
                    And nose and ears and hands and feet -
                    It seems to me you're quite complete!
                    Next, become a little braver -
                    Let me   try your lips for warmth and flavour;
                    Come and   my
                        But the best of all, just say "I will",
                          And then I'll get to know you better.
                    If I have permission to hold your hand,
                    I'll be in position to understand.
                    That experiment we will repeat,
                    Though my heart's just gone and missed a beat!
                    Now your pretty head on my shoulder place.
                    It is very nice being face to face -
                    Sort of makes me want to talk in rhyme
                    Just as though this were a pantomime.

                    Come about a half-inch nearer, etc.   ) - Together.)
                    If I have permission to hold your hand, etc.)

(They exit L.   Enter SQUIRE R, with a hand clasped to R. side of his
face.)

SQUIRE: Confound that beastly barber, he's completely destroyed my
image - well, half of it, anyway.   (Moves hand away and reveals that
R. side of his moustache has gone.)   Slipped with the razor, indeed!
And just because I asked for a little rent.   (Takes out large bottle labelle
"SILVIKRIN".)   I wonder if this stuff's any good?   (Takes a swig.)   Ugh
No!   Tastes disgusting.   (Throws bottle off D.L.)

HARDY: (off L)   OW!

(Enter HARDY and FOOLHARDY on scooter.   HARDY in a very long
haired wig.)

Somebody threw a bottle of Silvikrin at me.

SQUIRE: Never mind, nip to the barber and ask him for some rent. He'll give you a free haircut.

HARDY: Righto, papa. (Runs off R.)

SQUIRE: Now, Foolhardy.

(HARDY runs on R, without wig.)

SQUIRE: That was quick.

HARDY: Well, I found a short cut.

SQUIRE: So I see. Now listen, lads, I may need your help to evict Red Riding Hood.

HARDY &
FOOLHARDY: Evict Red Riding Hood?

HARDY: But she's our pretty little distant cousin.

SQUIRE: I know and I mean to make her your pretty little near mother.

FOOLHARDY: What's a near mother?

SQUIRE: One who's just a step away.

FOOLHARDY: Ah, a stepmother.

SQUIRE: Exactly. Now go and wait in the barn and come out when I clap my hands. Like this - (Claps them once, assisted by bonk from DRUMMER.)

HARDY &
FOOLHARDY: When you clap your hands. Yes, papa.

(They go into Barn leaving scooter D.L.   HARDY pokes head out.)

HARDY: I say, did you know you'd only got half a moustache?

SQUIRE: Only too well. Get in the barn.

(HARDY goes.)

(feeling upper lip) Hm, this might make wooing rather tricky. Ah, I have it - a touch of toothache. That'll make her feel sorry for me too.

(RED RIDING HOOD opens door as he raises hand to knock. He hurriedly puts it to L. side of his face.)

BOTH: Oh!

SQUIRE: Ah, dear cousin, pardon my hand - a slight toothache, I
      fear.

R. R. H. :   Oh, poor Squire, and I thought you'd called about the rent.
      Is that why you've shaved off your moustache?

SQUIRE: What?   (Moves hand to examine other side of lip and realises
      error.)

      (RED RIDING HOOD stifles a giggle.)

      (aside) Curses! (Angrily smacks fist on palm.   Bonk from DRUMMER
      HARDY and FOOLHARDY run on from barn.)

HARDY &
FOOLHARDY: Ready, papa.

SQUIRE: Well, I'm not.   Go away.

      (They go.)

SQUIRE: Now, my dear, since you mention it, there is the little
      matter of the rent.

R. R. H. :   (sighs) Oh well, I suppose I'll just have to sell my sheep.

SQUIRE: Sell your sheep?   Ah, no, let me help you out of your
      troubles.   (Kneels.)

      (SHEEP enter L. and move in between them.)

      Red Riding Hood - .

SHEEP: Baa.

SQUIRE: Oh get out of it.

      (SHEEP move D. L. and examine scooter with interest.)

SQUIRE: (clasping hands passionately and loudly together.   Bonk from
      DRUMMER) Red Riding Hood - .

HARDY &
FOOLHARDY: Ready, papa.

SQUIRE: No, you're too soon, go away!

SHEEP: (get on scooter and scoot off D. R)

HARDY &
FOOLHARDY: Hey, look -

SQUIRE: Go a-way!

(They shrug and go.)

Now where was I?

R.R.H: Red Riding Hood.

SQUIRE: Ah, yes. Red Riding Ho - (Almost claps hands together
again but realises and stops himself.) Hood, will you marry me and keep
your name to ours?

R.R.H: I'm sorry, Squire, but the answer's -

(BO PEEP rushes on L, and runs between them to R.)

BO PEEP: Baa!

SQUIRE: The answer's baa?

BO PEEP: Baa-Baa! The sheep! They've gone again.

SQUIRE: Tcha! The answer's what did you say?

(POPPET runs on L, and between them to BO PEEP.)

POPPET: Bo Peep! It's all right, I've organised search parties.

(They run back between them and off L. SQUIRE claps hand to forehead
in despair. Bonk from DRUMMER. HARDY & FOOLHARDY run on.)

HARDY &
FOOLHARDY: Ready, papa.

SQUIRE: No, you fools! I havn't found out the answer yet.

(They run off again.)

R.R.H: I'm afraid the answer's "no" Squire.

SQUIRE: Very well, I shall not shilly shally. Or shall I? Tcha!
You force me to take stern measures. I shall evict you. (Strides to barn.)

POPPET: (off L) Search parties, advance! Wuff! Wuff!

(SQUIRE claps hands loudly bonk from DRUMMER as a great barking
breaks out & POPPET enters with BO PEEP & CHORUS from L and form
into four groups, two of which search barking U.S. L. & R. and two D.S.
L. & R. SQUIRE claps again more loudly (louder bonks) then gives gesture
of resignation and bellows into barn.)

SQUIRE: HARDY!   FOOLHARDY!

(They run on)

HARDY &
FOOLHARDY: Ready, papa.

SQUIRE: About time too.   Evict her.

BOTH: (cupping hands to ears) Pardon, papa?

SQUIRE: E-vict her!

BOTH: Yes, papa.   (They take a step to do so, then stop.)

HARDY: We can't, papa.

SQUIRE: Why not?

HARDY: 'Cos she's outside already.

SQUIRE: Don't quibble over technicalities.   Take her in and bring
her out again.

(They shrug and mover to her as DAME TROT enters L.)

DAME: Whatever's happening? Has the dogs' Home caught fire?

R.R.H: No, it's all right, Granny, I'm just being evicted.

DAME: Oh, how nice for you, my dear - what?   Evicted?

R.R.H: Why can't you give me a little time to pay, Squire?   Then I
could sell my sheep?

SQUIRE: What sheep?   Surely you can hear - they're lost.   (Rubs
hands gleefully.)

(SHEEP enter D.R. on scooter and crash into him.)

SHEEP: Baa!

POPPET: Cease searching!

(Barking stops and groups stay still)

SQUIRE: Oh - fiddlesticks!

(Laughter and chatter break out, BO PEEP moves down to SHEEP
with POPPET.)

BO PEEP: Oh, you naughty, naughty, things.

SQUIRE: Nevertheless, the eviction will continue. Lads!

(PRINCE enters R, with axe on shoulder.)

PRINCE: Stop! The eviction will not continue.

SQUIRE: Oh, and who are you?

PRINCE: (moving to him) I, sir? I am just a woodcutter - with a very sharp axe. (Brings axe from shoulder.)

HARDY &
FOOLHARDY: (running behind SQUIRE. In small voices) The eviction will not continue.

SQUIRE: (gulps and backs in a circle D.S. to R.) I - I've just remembered, it's not rent day at all. No, not for some weeks, months - years! (Breaks into a run and jumps on scooter. Scooting off D.R.) Come, lads!

HARDY &
FOOLHARDY: (running after him) Coming, papa.

(SQUIRE returns and bumps into them.)

SQUIRE: Oops. (Aside.) I forgot to say - curse him!

(He scoots off R. and HARDY AND FOOLHARDY run after him.)

DAME: Well, this calls for a celebration. Let's have a party.

R.R.H: Yes, and it can be my birthday party.

DAME: Ah, or course! Your eighteenth birthday! My dear, I have something very important to tell you which - which I've forgotten. (To AUDIENCE.) Reminder, please.

(AUDIENCE shout. Forget-me-not grows a little and reveals another leaf. She crosses and picks leaf. Plant subsides)

Thank you. (Nibbles leaf.) That's it - you're an heirless - I mean an heiress.

ALL: What? An heiress! Etc. -)
) together.
R.R.H: An heiress, Granny?)

DAME: Yes, dear, there's a will which leaves you all the Hood
fortunes (Finishes leaf.) hidden away in - in - Oh dear, they're such small
leaves. Never mind, I'll find out when it grows another one. Meanwhile,
let's get on with the party!

ALL: Hooray!

MUSIC 16. "WHAT A LOVELY MORNING" (Reprise.)

> Oh, what a lovely morning
>   When a song we're sharing
>   And our voices airing.
> Oh, what a lovely morning
>   When each local yokel
>   Feels extremely vocal.
> We burst into song without reason,
> Merely because it's the silly season.
> Oh, what a lovely morning
>   To be singing, singing, singing in the sun.

BLACKOUT.

(Close traverse tabs. Fly in Scene Two frontcloth.)

ACT ONE

SCENE TWO - A WOODLAND GLADE

(MUSIC 17. WHITE FLASH R. and WHITE SPOT up R. revealing the
DOWAGER FAIRY DUTIFUL, carrying a wand and wearing a highly
ornamental pair of lorgnettes and a pendant watch.)

FAIRY: Your pardon if I did surprise.
You see, not as you might surmise,
Some mystic vision beautiful,
But me, the Fairy Dutiful. (Curtsies.)
A Dowager Fairy I should stress,
One of the Little People, yes.
But now I fear I'm all behind -
A figure of speech was i n my mind -
We Fairies should guard two at most,
But I'm the Guardian to a host -
I've babes - a pair, and pigs - a threesome,
I've Cinderella and her besom,
Plus Mother Goose and Snow White too
And even then I've nam'd but few.
But now I've come to do some good
Unto my ward, Red Riding Hood.
What's happen'd since I saw her last?
(Raises lorgnettes to her eyes.)
Through these I can survey the past.
Ooh! What a murky past it's been -
Oh no, of course, they need a clean.
(Wipes lorgnettes and looks through them again.)
Ah! Who's this she's met? Florizel?
Why, he's a ward of mine as well.
Splendid!   The pair shall wed and thus
Save me not only time, but fuss.
(Looks through lorgnettes again.)
But wait, the Prince is hinder'd by
Some tiresome curse to make him shy.
Ah, Demon's work. But which one is't?
Let's see the Demon's fixture list.
(Takes a card from her bosom and consults it.)
Oh, Sheerspite. Hardly worth my mettle
He's harmless as a stinging nettle.

(MUSIC 18. GREEN FLASH L. & GREEN SPOT up L, which DEMON
SHEERSPITE leaps into.)

DEMON: What'th thith? Who takth my name in vain?
Tho, foolith fairy - thee again!
Dotht dare onth more to routh my power?

FAIRY: Yes, but I'd hop'd without the shower.

DEMON: Thy mocking worth have theal'd thy fate;
              Now I'll my fury not abate
              Till to the dutht you cruthed be!
              'Tith through thy wardth I'll ruin thee -
              To luckleth endth I'll thpeed pell mell
              Red Riding Hood and Florithel
              And thuth thy loathethome might dethtroy!

FAIRY: Don't spray me with your threats, dear boy.
              Such boasts from you before I've heard,
              But seen no deed to match a word,
              So please - (Music ting. She puts hand to ear,
                        Ah, Cinderella's call.
              (looks at watch.)
              Yes, time that child went to a ball.
              I'll have to fly. A word though first -
              Do try your best to do your worst!

        (Exit FAIRY R.   WHITE SPOT OUT.)

DEMON: Well, jutht for that 'twould therve her right
              If I did nothing out of thpite.
              But that'th a rithk I dare not take;
              My reputation ith at thtake -
              Folk won't believe my evil worth
              Becauthe I lithp, it'th thuch a curth!
              I've one latht chanth to prove mythelf
              Or be demoted to an elf!
              Tho to work - firtht, Red Riding Hood!
              There livth a wolf within the wood
              And he thall theal her fate for me.
              But thith motht thubtly done mutht be
              Or Dutiful will thmell a rat.
              But I know how to get round that -
              I'll gull the Thquire to work my plan,
              And here he comth - the very man.

        (Enter SQUIRE R.)

SQUIRE: Oh, fiddlesticks! And like rude words,
              My life's like cream that's turn'd to curds,
              My hope's like so much runny whey -

DEMON: In fact, you're "Cheeth'd off" one might thay.

SQUIRE: (fixes a baleful eye on DEMON) And who are you, may I
  enquire?

DEMON: Theerthpite'th my name.   Greetingth, Thir Thquire.

SQUIRE: Sheerspit, you say?

DEMON: No, no, Theerthpite.

SQUIRE: (mopping himself with hanky). I still think in a way I'm
    right.

DEMON: I've come to aid thee.

SQUIRE: Oh, indeed?

DEMON: Yeth, I know jutht the thing you need.

SQUIRE: That's several things my coz - some cash
            Besides one half of my moustache.

DEMON: The last I'll deal with in a trithe. (Bottle flies in, music
    whizz - or DEMON produces it gives it to SQUIRE.)

SQUIRE: Some hair restorer.   Well, how nice.

DEMON: And magic.   For thy coth, though, Thquire
            A wolf'th the thing that

SQUIRE: A wolf?

DEMON: Yeth, thinth thy troubleth thtem -
            From thilly theep - a pair of them.

SQUIRE: I may be dense, but what are theep?

DEMON: Thoth thingth you count when you can't thleep.
            With fleetheth.

SQUIRE: Fleetheth?

DEMON: Yeth, of wool.

SQUIRE: Are you trying my leg to pull?
            First wolves, now sheep - my mind's a-muzz.
            How will sheep help to win my coz?

DEMON: Well, if her theep were thtolen - gone.

SQUIRE: She'd be more easily put upon!

DEMON: And for the theft what better than
            A fearthome wolf? And one that can
            Be told jutht what to do and where
            Thinth he'th a kind of wolf motht rare,
            For I have taught him how to thpeak.

SQUIRE: He sounds the very thing I seek!

DEMON: I'm glad you like my little thcheme.

SQUIRE: It's just exactly on my beam.
I always say to gain success
There's nought succeeds like wickedness.

MUSIC 19 - "BE BAD"

BOTH: If you aspire to rise in your profession,
  Just take this word of good advice from us -
That wickedness is your most prized possession -
  You'll find that you'll be better if you're wuss!
If neighbours turn out sensitive, as neighbours often are,
And make complaints at midnight when you're tuning up the
                                                    car,
Just go into a shop and buy an amplified guitar -
          That's the secret - be bad.'
If you should own a cosh or knuckle-duster
  And want to have a little bit of fun,
Just break as many heads as you can muster,
  And what is more, you'll be a man, my son!
When you get tired of using awf'lly awful words like "damn",
And feeding tots of whisky to a baby in a pram,
It's lovely fun to fill a person's shoes with raspberry jam -
          That's the secret - be bad!
Sell your sister's jewels for eighteen pence;
Draw moustaches on advertisements;
Put your tongue out at the local cop;
Then in the ending you'll be descending to the top!
Good deeds - it would be better if you missed 'em;
Good deeds can make the worst intentions faint;
They gradually impregnate the system
  And turn the vilest sinner to a saint.
So keep on keeping on with all the evil things you do,
Like singing all the pops, and smearing telephones with glue;
Then one fine day there'll be a seat in Parliament for you -
          That's the secret - be bad!

See "X" films before you're in your teens;
Put bent pennies in the slot machines;
Lame the other fellows in the race -
You'll get ahead if only you tread on someone's face!
If entertainment is the thing you're seeking,
  Then damaging the district is the thing;
Go smash with stones that old Belisha Beaking,
  And use your father's braces as a sling.
The moral of this ballad isn't very hard to find -
Make sure you take advantage of the people who are kind!
If you don't push yourself in front you might get left behind -
          That's the secret - be bad!

                    BLACKOUT.
(Open traverse tabs.)

ACT ONE

SCENE THREE - THE WOLF'S LAIR IN THE FOREST

(Fullset. Ground row cut-out representing woodland scene at back of rostrum. Woodwings L. & R. A sloping bank cut-out piece coming on-stage from R. wing. U.C. in front of rostrum a sort of hillock in which is a low rough wooden doorway, with practical door. A knocker on the door and a grass mat in front of it. Inscribed on a board above the door is "THE LUPINS". To one side of doorway a nameplate with a sliding In-Out panel, which at present reads "A. LUPE - OUT". On the other side of doorway is a small window. Log. L.C.

There is a growl off R. MUSIC 20. LUPE the wolf pokes his head on R. looks round, then nips on, runs to door and tries to open it, then bangs head with a paw.)

LUPE: Fool - it's locked.

(Lifts up a corner of grass mat and pickes up key from underneath it, opens door, replaces key, wipes hind-paws carefully on mat, then steps inside doorway and turns to wipe forepaws, moves panel over to "IN" and shuts door. Slight pause. Window opens and a paw shakes out a duster. Slight pause again and the door opens and LUPE, now wearing a little apron and wielding a broom, sweeps some dust out of the front door.)

LUPE: There, that's done. That's the worst of being a lone wolf - you have to do your own housework. (Puts broom inside house and yawns) I'm tired. I've been out hunting for hours, no luck though, so I'll have to make-do with a nut cutlet again. Ugh. And I hate nuts. I only like meat. Roast lamb now - yummy-yum-yum! Or people - Especially people pudding. Ooh, scrumptious!

DAME: (off L.) Come along, dears, this way.

LUPE: Ooh, here comes a people now, what luck! I'll tear up an old sheet for a pudding bag. (Runs into house.)

(Enter DAME TROT L.)

DAME: Yes, this is the way, dears. (Turns.) Oh, no dears. And, anyway, where were we going? Ah. (To AUDIENCE.) Reminder, please.

(AUDIENCE reaction. Forget-me-not grows and reveals another leaf.)

Thank you, and there it is, such a handy little plant - grows everywhere. (Crosses to forget-me-not.)

(As she does so, LUPE opens door holding a sheet and measures her with his eye.)

LUPE: Ha, a bit too big.

(DAME bends to get a leaf and LUPE tears a strip from sheet. DAME freezes, smiles unce rtainly at AUDIENCE, and puts a hand to her behind to examine damage.)

LUPE: Still too big.

(DAME gingerly straightens up and has almost reached half-way before LUPE tears again, this time tearing in jerks as if it is more difficult and DAME finishes rise in a series of jerks. Plant subsides.)

DAME: Funny, I can't feel a draught anywhere. Still excuse me a moment, will you. (Sidles sideways to L. as BO PEEP enters L.)

BO PEEP: Baa! Baa-Baa!

LUPE: Oh, goody, two peoples! I'll make another pudding—bag. (Disappears into house.)

DAME: Ah, Bo Peep, would you just look and see - have I got a tear round the bottom of my dress?

BO PEEP: (walking round behind her to her R, looking) No, I can't see one.

DAME: Strange, Ah, well. I say, wasn't Red Riding Hood with us when we started out?

BO PEEP: Yes, but she went along another path to look for Baa and Baa-Baa. You see ... I - er - well, I'm not exactly sure where they are

DAME: Where what are, dear?

(LUPE re-appears with another sheet.)

BO PEEP: My sheep.

LUPE: (in delight) Sheep!

DAME: I know you've got two sheep, dear.

LUPE: Two sheep!

DAME: Funny sort of echo round here. Let's sit down and wait for Red Riding Hood.   (DAME and BO PEEP start to sit on log L. C. as LUP tears a strip off the sheet and they remain stuck half-way down in mid-air looking rather startled. Both feel their posteriors gingerly and smile weakly at each other.)

Lovely day, isn't it?

BO PEEP: Lovely.

(They start to lower themselves very slowly.)

LUPE: Absolutely ripping!

(Tears sheet again. BO PEEP and DAME sink hurriedly down with a bump.)

DAME: I shall have to go on a diet.

BO PEEP: So shall I.

LUPE: I shan't (Rubs tummy happily and disappears into house.)

R.R.H.   (off L) Baa! Baa-Baa!

BO PEEP: (starting to jump up, but thinking better of it and sitting again) Ah, Red Riding Hood.

(Enter RED RIDING HOOD L.)

Oh, dear, haven't you found them either?

R.R.H: (sitting on end of log) No, but I expect they're only playing hide and seek in the woods. Oughtn't we to be getting on, Granny? It'll be getting dark soon.

DAME: Oh, yes, dear. Er - where to?

R.R.H: I don't know. You were taking us to wherever this will is hidden.

(LUPE re-enters from house wearing a cook's hat and butcher's apron.)

LUPE: Three peoples! Well, I'll just pinch them to see which is the most tender. (Moves behind them. He pinches RED RIDING HOOD on R. side with a forepaw and nods.)

R.R.H: Ooh! Was that you, Granny?

DAME: Was that me, what, dear?

(LUPE pinches her on R. side and shakes head.)

Ow! (To BO PEEP.) Did you want something, dear?

BO PEEP: Who, me?

(LUPE pinches her on R. side and nods.)

Ouch (Turning to her R.) Did you - oh.

LUPE: (pointing to BO PEEP and RED RIDING HOOD) Eeny-meeny
miny-mo, catch a nigger by his toe,

OTHER 3:   (joining in) If he hollers let him go, eeny-meeny-miny-mo.
(They go too fast and confuse him.)

DAME: What are we doing this for?

LUPE: Just to get me all confused.

OTHER 3:   Sorry. Eh?

LUPE: Well, I'll have you. (Puts head between DAME and R.R.H.)

BO & DAME: (turning to each other))
)   What?
R.R.H: (turning to DAME)   )

          (RED RIDING HOOD screams, jumps up and runs off L.   LUPE
          straightens up in annoyance. BO PEEP and DAME stare out front
          startled.)

LUPE: All right, you. (Puts head between DAME and BO PEEP.)

BO & DAME: (turning to look L.) Beg pardon?

          (BO PEEP screams, jumps up and runs off R. LUPE again   straightens
          up annoyed. DAME swings round to R.)

DAME: Where's everybody got to? (Rises and moves round in a
circle with LUPE behind her until she faces front again.)

               Do you ever get the feeling when you're all alone that you're
not? 'Cos I've got it now.   I mean, I am alone, aren't I? (AUDIENCE
reaction.) What? I'm not? Are you sure? (AUDIENCE reaction)
But there's nobody there. (Turns L.) And there's nobody there.
(Turns R.) What? Behind me? (Turns and comes face to face with LUPE.
Turns back.) No, there's nobody there, either - except a wolf.
AAAAAAAHHHHHHHHH.' (Picks up skirts and belts off L.)

LUPE: Oh, how sickening. (Takes off apron and cap and throws
them into house.) I did want one of them to stay for dinner.   You see -

          MUSIC 21. I LIKE PEOPLE.

LUPE: I like people, tender little people.
               Be they tiny or tall, be they fat or just slender little people;
                    Teenagers in tight dress,
                    Children in their night-dress,
                    I have just the right rec-
                         -ipe.'

I adore them, simply just adore them.
I would like them to know there is nothing that I would
                    not do for them.
    It's a matter of taste that people should haste
    To be in my company -
            Why don't people like me?

When I meet them, I could really eat them!
If it's ever a matter of something in batter none can beat
                                    them.
    Though I burst at the seams with marvellous schemes
    For making a fricassee,
    Why don't people - tasty little people,
            Why don't people like me?

(LUPE goes into his house and shuts door. Slight pause. Enter HARDY and FOOLHARDY disguised as two trees R.)

FOOLHARDY: Oi!

HARDY: Ssh!

FOOLHARDY: But I want to talk to you.

HARDY: Don't be silly, Foolhardy, trees can't talk.

FOOLHARDY: All right, then - woof-woof!

HARDY: What do you mean - woof-woof? You're not a dog, you're a tree.

FOOLHARDY: Well, that was the bark of a tree. Anyway, if we can't talk to each other, we could make signs by waving a boojer.

HARDY: Waving a boojer? What's a boojer?

FOOLHARDY: You know, one of these - (Waves arm in bough.) a b-o-u-g-h- boojer.

HARDY: That's not pronounced boojer.

FOOLHARDY: No?

HARDY: No. Bough.

FOOLHARDY: I can't.

HARDY: Can't what?

FOOLHARDY: Bow. Not in this. I might manager a curtsey, though.

HARDY: Look, Papa told us to find those two new woodcutters and keep an eye on them.   Let's get on with it.

(Sounds of chopping of L.)

Ah, there they are now.   One of 'em's chopping down a tree.

FOOLHARDY: Then let's go before they try to chop us down.

HARDY: No, stay still and keep quiet.

(FOOLHARDY does.   Chopping stops.)

POPPET: (off L.)   Timber!

(Crash of tree falling.)

Ow, (Enters L. rubbing head.) Well, how was I to know it would fall that way.

(Enter PRINCE.)

PRINCE: Bad luck, Poppet.   Still I expect practice makes perfect. (Leans with an arm against HARDY.)

POPPET: It also makes you jolly sore. (Leans with an arm against FOOLHARDY.)

Oh, by the way, sir, about the Squire. (Moves to PRINCE.)

PRINCE: (moving to POPPET.)   Yes?

(TREES shuffle round behind them listening eagerly.)

POPPET: I havn't found out anything yet.

PRINCE: Oh.   Well, neither have I.

POPPET: Ah. (Steps back to lean against HARDY and as he is not there nearly falls over.)

PRINCE: What's the matter Poppet?

POPPET: I thought I was leaning against a tree here.

PRINCE: You were, and I was leaning against one (Turns.) here.

(HARDY just manages to get back into place before PRINCE turns.)

POPPET: (turning to PRINCE) That's right. Well then, where's my (Turns.) oh.

(FOOLHARDY just manages to get back into place before POPPET turns to him.)

But the branches looked different before.   More like - (Turns away miming FOOLHARDY'S previous arm position.   FOOLHARDY hastily rearranges arms.)

PRINCE: Um?   (Turns to POPPET.)   But they are like that.

POPPET: (miming FOOLHARDY'S second arm position)   No, they're like this.   (Turns.   Scratches head, puzzled.)   Perhaps these would make a couple of good trees to practice some more woodcutting on.

PRINCE: Good idea.

(As PRINCE and POPPET prepare themselves to swing their axes HARDY and FOOLHARDY exchange horrified looks then turn and run off, HARDY L. and FOOLHARDY R.)

BOTH: Now then -   (They turn back to where trees were and exchange a look of astonishment.)

POPPET: Somebody's beaten us to it.

PRINCE: I think we've seen so many trees today we're beginning to imagine them.   We'd better make an early night of it.

POPPET: Yes, sir.   Where?

PRINCE: Where?   Here.   We'll sleep on the ground.   What could be better than that?

POPPET :   A nice soft mattress and a hot water bottle.

MUSIC 22.   "ISN'T IT SURPRISING".

PRINCE :   I could sleep beneath the weeping willow.

POPPET: I prefer a mattress and a pillow.

PRINCE: He tells lies -

POPPET: And he pretends -

BOTH: Isn't it surprising that we're such good friends!

PRINCE :   I would like a sandwich and a cuppa

POPPET: I shall go to Claridges* for supper.

PRINCE: He talks tripe -

POPPET: And he eats worms!

BOTH: Isn't it surprising we're on speaking terms!

PRINCE: I like black -

POPPET: I like white.

PRINCE: I like day -

POPPET: And I like night.

BOTH: If you'd live in harmony
You must agree to disagree.

POPPET: My suit's cut in Saville Row, that's certain.

PRINCE: Mine comes from the Dorking* branch of Burton.

POPPET: Go to Mayfair*!

PRINCE: Go to (Cough.).

BOTH: Isn't it surprising we get on so well!

PRINCE: I like this -

POPPET: And I like that!

PRINCE: Blow for blow -

POPPET: And tit for tat!

BOTH: If on all we quite agreed
We would be very dull indeed.

PRINCE: I would like to bang you on the beezer!

POPPET: I would like to smite you on the sneezer!

BOTH: That's the way it always ends.
Isn't it surprising -

PRINCE: Utterly amazing!

POPPET: Absolutely Stunning -

BOTH: That we're such good friends!

(*Suitable local allusions - which scan can be substituted.)

(They lie down behind sloping piece U. R.   MUSIC 23.   Enter FAIRY
DUTIFUL R, carrying a large steak.)

FAIRY: Well, I've sent Cinders off in style,
                  So that's one dealt with for a while.
                  But now to save Prince Florizel,
                  Not to mention his page as well.
                  For here they lie, the foolish pair,
                  Asleep beside a lupine lair.
                  This steak I've brought to put things right
                  And blunt the wolfish appetite.

(Puts steak down, R.of doorway.)

                  It were as well, while I am here,
                  To see no other danger's near.

(Looks through lorgnettes.)

                  What's this? Oh, no! What perfidy!
                  The wolf will with the sheep make free
                  And then 'tis Sheerspite's plan he should
                  Just gobble up Red Riding Hood!
                  Well, what a liberty to take!
                  I'll put a spell upon this steak.

(LIGHTS DIM.   MUSIC 24.   FAIRY waves wand over steak.)

                  Steak, o'er thee I magic baste,
                  Let the wolf take but one taste
                  And gone will be his savage state
                  Replac'd by one that's more sedate.

(LIGHTS UP.   MUSIC dies.)

                  There. (Music ting.) Ooh, another call, I trow.
                  A fairy's life is just all go.
                  Jack Durden 'tis that needs me now.
                  He wants, I think, to sell a cow.

(Exit R.   Enter HARDY L & FOOLHARDY R.   They collide in C, and both
freeze hastily into their tree positions, then slowly their faces come up
and see each other.)

BOTH: Oh, it's you.

FOOLHARDY: I told you those woodcutters might try to cut us down.

HARDY: Well, that's an occupational risk with trees.

(LUPE yawns loudly in house.)

Look out! Somebody else!

(They freeze into their tree positions again. LUPE appears yawning and stretching wearing a nightcap.)

LUPE: Ah, I feel better for that little nap. (Sniffs.) Ooh, I can smell steak, luscious. (Tracks it with his nose, then looks up sniffing.) Um. Better still - I can smell peoples. (Tracks scent until he is between HARDY and FOOLHARDY.) People trees? Impossible!

FOOLHARDY: (whispering and nudging HARDY) Hey, Hardy, I think it's a dog.

HARDY: Well?

FOOLHARDY: Well, we're trees.

(LUPE sniffs at them.)

HARDY: I see what you mean.

FOOLHARDY: What shall we do?

HARDY: Uproot ourselves!

(They run off L. LUPE looks after them in astonishment, then shrugs.)

LUPE: Well, I suppose people trees would be able to run. Pity though. (Sniffs.) Never mind, here comes a people people. Looks a bit tough, I'd better mince him, I think. (Runs into house. Enter SQUIRE R, mopping his face with a hanky. His moustache is complete again.)

SQUIRE: Five hundred and eighty-seven, five hundred and eighty-eight, five hundred and eighty-nine. Ah, this must be the spot. Meet me by the five hundred and eighty-ninth tree on the left, Sheerspite said. (Stroking moustache.) His magic hair restorer's worked very well. But where is he? I don't fancy meeting the wolf without him.

(Enter LUPE from house with a mincing machine.)

LUPE: Good evening.   Waiting for somebody?

SQUIRE: Yes.

LUPE: (turning handle) Let me press you to a little mince while you're waiting then.

SQUIRE: That's very kind of you but I think Demon Sheerspite will be -

LUPE: Oh, no, don't say he's coming here. He'll expect me to do a lot of tomfool tricks, just because he taught me how to talk.

SQUIRE: Taught you to talk? Really? Well, I know he taught - HELP! (Runs L. There is a GREEN FLASH L, GREEN SPOT UP cymbal crash and DEMON leaps on.)

DEMON: It'th all right, Thquire, no need to fear,
No harm shall come now I am here.
Good wolf, Lupe, thit.

(LUPE sits begrudgingly.)

Now raithe your paw.
Thay how d'ye do.

LUPE: (aside) Oh, what a bore. (Unwillingly offers paw, which SQUIRE takes even more unwillingly and shakes very hastily.)

DEMON: Thee? Underthtandth each word I thay.
What'th that?

(Crosses to steak and picks it up.)

Thome thteak. How, lucky, eh!
For now you'll thee hith favourite trick.
Beg.

(LUPE shrugs resignedly and begs. DEMON puts steak on LUPE'S hand.)

Patienth.

(LUPE growls very impatiently.)

Paid for!

(LUPE flicks steak into air and catches it in mouth or forepaws.)

SQUIRE: Very slick!

DEMON: He lovth hith food, jutht watch him eat

(LUPE tears into steak savagely. MUSIC ting. LUPE stops eating in a disgusted way.)

LUPE: Ugh! Funny, I've gone right off meat.   (Suddenly bounds about the stage like a playful puppy.   DEMON and SQUIRE exchange surprised looks.)

SQUIRE: His manner's surely rather rum.

LUPE: (lying down, kicking legs in air)
            Give me a tickle on my tum.

DEMON: Enough, Lupe, theath thith idle play,
            I've work for you, litht what I thay.

      (LUPE sits.)

            Within the wood there are two theep.

LUPE: Yes, so I heard from one Bo Peep.

DEMON: Well, 'tith thy tathk the pair to thteal
            And then their hapleth fate to theal.

LUPE: Oh, no! I couln't. Well, I could,
            But do you really think I should?

DEMON: Of courth you thould when I thay tho.

LUPE: Oh, very well, but one thing, though.
            I quite refuse the sheep to kill.

DEMON: You mutht!

LUPE: I won't.

DEMON: Yes, yes, you will.

LUPE: To argue more I'll not demean.

DEMON: Thith ith a thnag I'd not fortheen.
            Thuch thtubborneth! Oh, I could thwear!
            We'll have to hide 'em then, but where?

SQUIRE: I know - Hood Hall, where none dare goes,
            For 'tis haunted, as they suppose.

DEMON: Yeth, thuch a thpot were hard to beat.
            At midnight then there let uth meet.
            So hurry, Lupe.

LUPE: All right, hold on.
            I've hunting-sheep-type-kit to don.

(Exit into house.)

SQUIRE: (moving R)
I'll find my sons to help us, too.

DEMON: Farewell for now.

SQUIRE: Yes, toodle-oo

(Exit SQUIRE R. & DEMON L.   Enter LUPE from house wearing a little sheepskin and carrying a little fishing-rod with a large bottle labelled "MINT SAUCE" on its line.)

LUPE: There, the perfect disguise. It's a pity my sheepskin's shrunk, but wool is tricky to wash, isn't it?   Still, it'll fool a couple of silly sheep.   And here's my sheep catcher. (Shows fishing rod. Moving down L. side of stage, holding out fishing rod.) Sheep, sheep, sheep, sheep! (Moves across front.) Sheep, sheep! Sheep, sheep!

(MUSIC 25. BAA and BAA-BAA enter L and halt when they see LUPE. BAA makes to run away but BAA-BAA stops her and they watch LUPE as he continues calling and moving to R. side of stage. BAA-BAA points a hoof to his head to indicate that LUPE is obviously mad and BAA nods agreement.   LUPE is now bending slightly looking off R.   BAA-BAA nudges BAA, lowers his head and runs across to butt LUPE in the behind and knock him over.   BAA hastily puts a hoof to her mouth to stifle her laughter.   End MUSIC.)

LUPE: (rising and turning) Who did that?   Who -

BAA-BAA: (points to himself) Baa!

LUPE: You?   But you're a sheep.   Don't you realise I'm a wolf?

BAA-BAA: (shakes head and points to LUPE'S sheepskin)

LUPE: Ah, that fooled you, eh?   Well, I'm a wolf in sheep's clothing, so I bet you wouldn't dare butt me to my face.

BAA-BAA: (nods, lowers head and obligingly butts LUPE in stomach)

LUPE: (falling over) Ow!

BAA: Ba-ha-ha-ha-ha!

LUPE: (turning and seeing BAA) And don't you laugh.   Oh, another sheep.   Two sheeps.   Just what I'm looking for.   I'm going to steal you.

(The SHEEP look surprised then shake their heads.)

LUPE: (rising with bottom towards BAA) Yes, I am.

BAA-BAA: (BAA-BAA butts him in bottom.   LUPE is propelled forward towards BAA who butts him in stomach)

LUPE: Ow! Ooh! STOP IT! Two onto one, it's not fair.

(BO PEEP enters R.)

BO PEEP: Baa! Baa-Baa!

SHEEP: (running and hiding behind L.)   Baa!

LUPE: Ah, a people to protect me.   (Running to her.)   Please -

BO PEEP: (screams.   Runs off R.)   AAAAH! Help! The wolf! Help, help! The wolf!

LUPE: You just can't rely on people.   Now come here, you two.

SHEEP: (shake their heads and run L.)

LUPE: (aside)   All right, if I can't force 'em, I'll fool 'em.   (To them) Bet you can't catch me-ee!

(They immediately chase after him.   MUSIC 26.   He circles clockwise D.S.)

LUPE: See?   I knew they'd follow.   They're just like sheep.

(As they pass house.   ALL mark time a moment as he slides panel to "OUT" and then run off.   MUSIC ends.   BO PEEP runs on R. followed by CHORUS.

BO PEEP: Oh, hurry, hurry!

CHORUS: What's the matter, Bo Peep?   Why were you shouting help? What's all the fuss?   What's gone wrong?   What's happened?   What is it?   Etc.

BO PEEP: Too late!   They've gone!

(POPPET and FLORIZEL wake and sit up.)

POPPET: Awfully noisy sort of forest this.

BO PEEP: Poppet!   )
) -(Together.)
CHORUS: The woodcutters!   )

(They move down.   Enter RED RIDING HOOD and DAME TROT R.)

DAME: Ah, there you are, Bo Peep.

R. R. H. :   We've been looking for you everywhere.

BO PEEP: Oh, Red Riding Hood, something awful's happened.   I've -
I've lost the sheep!

    (ALL laugh.)

BO PEEP: No, I mean really, really lost them this time.   The wolf's
stolen them!

    (Reaction from ALL.)

    So now, how can I ever find them?

    (MUSIC 27.   "LITTLE BO PEEP".)

ALL: Little Bo Peep
                Has lost her sheep
                And doesn't know where
                And doesn't know where to find them.
                Leave them alone
                And they'll come home
                Bringing their tails
                Bringing their tails
                Behind them
                Bringing their tails behind them.

                Little Bo Peep
                Has lost her sheep
                And doesn't know where to find them
                And doesn't know where to find them.
                Leave them alone
                And they'll come home
                Leave them alone
                And they'll come home
                Bringing their tails
                Their tails
                Their tails
                Their tails
                Behind them
                Bringing their tails behind them.

                Little Bo Peep
                Has lost her sheep
                And doesn't know where
                And doesn't know where to find them.

BLACKOUT
(Close traverse tabs.   Fly in Scene Four Frontcloth.)

ACT ONE

SCENE FOUR - ON THE WAY TO THE HAUNTED HOUSE

(Frontcloth, or tabs.   Cloth if used to represent a country road.   Open traverse tabs during scene as soon as cloth is in.   Old signpost pointing to "HOOD HALL"   placed in blackout.   Two hooks on signpost.)

(MUSIC 28.   HARDY runs on L. and FOOLHARDY R.)

FOOLHARDY: Ooh, thank goodness I've found you.   I've been having a terrible time.   Just look what's happened.   (Turns round to reveal a heart pierced by an arrow and "J.G. loves E.T." inscribed in the bark over his behind.)

HARDY: Hm, obviously gets around a bit this J.G.   Look.   (Turns round to reveal similar arrow pierced heart and the inscription "J.G. loves B.D." inscribed over his behind.   SQUIRE is heard singing off R.)

FOOLHARDY: Look out!   Somebody coming!

(Enter SQUIRE R.   They start to freeze into tree positions but relax on seeing who it is.)

HARDY: Oh, it's just papa.   Papa!

SQUIRE: Funny, I thought I heard somebody calling, but there's only a couple of tree trunks here.

FOOLHARDY: Well, we're making a trunk call.

SQUIRE: Oh.   (Takes FOOLHARDY'S R. hand and puts it to his ear and holds his L. hand to speak into.)   Hullo?   Sir False Hood speaking.

HARDY: Oh, papa, it's us - Hardy and Foolhardy.

SQUIRE: Ah, good.   Where are you speaking from?

HARDY: We're in disguise.

SQUIRE: Well, hurry back from there - and meet me at Hood Hall as soon as you can.   Oh, and bring some sheets with you, I've got a job for you.   Goodbye.   (Crossing L.)   I don't know, these lads get all over the place, nowadays.   (Exit SQUIRE L.)

FOOLHARDY: Now what do we do?

HARDY: What he says, I suppose.   Come on.   (Starts to move R.)

Hold it! Here comes that dog! This way.

(They run off L. Slight pause. Enter LUPE R.)

LUPE: Baa! Baa-Baa! Now, I've lost those blooming sheep.
And I've tried everything - even hoofcuffs. (Shows handcuffs attached to
each of his own wrists and the empty halves dangling free.) No good -

(SHEEP creep on R. BAA-BAA creeps behind him and squats close to
him on his L. BAA squats on his R, hiding a coil of rope behind her
back. Both are holding their tails in their mouths.)

One moment they're there and the next they're not. (Turns to move L
and falls over BAA-BAA. Straightening up.) You see what I mean?
Of course, I should have brought some rope to tie you two up.

(BAA offers coil from behind her back, which is looped at each end.)

Mm. I'm sure there's a catch in it somewhere, but I'll risk it.
(Holding out the loops.) You don't mind if I - ?

                    (SHEEP shake heads)

LUPE: (putting loops over them) Very odd. In fact, there's something strange about you two altogether. I know, don't you usually wear
those the other end?

                    (SHEEP nod)

LUPE: Perhaps I should try it. Does it hurt much?

                    (SHEEP shake heads)

LUPE: (tugging sharply at own tail, and clasps rear in pain) Ow!
Fibbers! (Picks up middle of rope and exits L, pulling them behind
him.) I should have know I'd regret it in the end.

(As they go off the SHEEP carefully hang their tails on the signpost.
Slight pause. HARDY looks on L.)

HARDY: It's all right, the dog's gone. (He enters and FOOLHARDY
follows him on.) Let's get home and get out of these things. (Is
moving R and suddenly wheels round and runs L.) Back again!

FOOLHARDY: (following) Now what?

HARDY: Woodcutters!

(They run off L. Sounds of barking off R and POPPET, BO PEEP,
FLORIZEL and RED RIDING HOOD run on barking.)

POPPET: (stopping suddenly) Stop!

BO PEEP: Why, have you found something?

POPPET: No, I've lost something.

BO PEEP: What?

POPPET: My breath.

R. R. H.:   I say, look!

ALL: LAMB'S TAILS! (They run to tails.)

BO PEEP: (taking them) They're theirs!

PRINCE: And obviously they put them there to show us where they've been taken.

BO PEEP: Ooh dear. Hood Hall! That's haunted. Somebody told me they went there one night and heard a sort of whispering among the trees.

R. R. H.:   It must have been the wind, then. Trees can't whisper.

FOOLHARDY: (off L.) I tell you I'm sick of being a tree.

HARDY: (off L.) But we can't strip off our bark here. It might upset all the other trees.

FOOLHARDY: (off) It'll upset me a lot more if we don't.

POPPET: I see what you mean - trees can't whisper, they just shout.

PRINCE: You'd better leave this to us. We're not afraid of trees and ghosts, are we, Poppet?

POPPET: Afraid? Of course not, just scared to death.

PRINCE: Nonsense. Come on. (Swings axe up to hold it purposefully in front of himself and exits L.)

POPPET: Goodbye. Forever. (Swings axe similarly and hits himself in face.) Ow! (Exit L.)

R. R. H.   Well, I'm certainly not afraid of ghosts and I think we ought to go there too.

BO PEEP: Oh, so do I - first thing in the morning.

R. R. H. :   No, I mean now, but if you're worried, I tell you what we'll do (Whispers in her ear.)

BO PEEP: Tablecloths?

R. R. H. :   Yes, large ones.   Come on, we'll go and get them.

(They start to go.   BO PEEP stops.)

BO PEEP: Oh dear, how awful.

R. R. H. :   What's awful about tablecloths?

BO PEEP: No, not tablecloths.   These.   (Holds up tails.)   I've just thought - now the poor little dears won't be able to come home bringing them behind them.

(They run off R.   HARDY and FOOLHARDY, now de-treed, enter.)

HARDY: Now we're safe.

DAME: (off R)   Hey, wait for me!

HARDY: No, we're not.   Freeze!

FOOLHARDY: But -

HARDY: Don't argue - freeze!

(They freeze into tree positions.   DAME TROT runs on R.)

DAME: Hold on!   (To HARDY and FOOLHARDY.)   Oh, hullo.   (No reaction.)   Whew!   I'm exhausted.   I haven't run as much as that since I won the under fives egg and spoon race and that's I don't know how many years ago.   At least, I do, but what's the use of a bad memory if it can't forget a little thing like that eh?   I said wh-   (Breaks off to move a hand before their eyes to see if they blink, and turns away.)   I wonder if they often get taken like this?   Now what was I running for?   Reminder, please.

(AUDIENCE shout.)

Thank you.

(Plant shoots up.)

Ah, such an obliging plant.   (Picks a leaf and takes a bite.   Plant subsides.)   Oh, of course, the sheep.   But wasn't there something else? (Takes another bite.)   Yes, the will - and it's hidden in Hood Hall! Behind - Oh dear, run out again.   Never mind.   On to Hood Hall. (Runs off L.)

FOOLHARDY: I say, why are we standing like this?

HARDY: Because we're trees.

FOOLHARDY: But we're not now.

HARDY: Eh? (Looks down at himself.) Oh. No. Yes. Well. We'd better go home and find those sheets for papa. I wonder why he wants us to bring sheets?

FOOLHARDY: Oh, something silly. He never asks us to do anything
sensible.   I can't think why not.

HARDY: Nor can I. But perhaps that's why - we just can't think.

(Close traverse tabs slowly during number. Fly out frontcloth. MUSIC
29. "NOTHING UPSTAIRS".)

BOTH: People sit thinking and thinking and thinking
                   And worry on current affairs;
               But that sort of fuss is quite foreign to us,
                   'Cos we know we've got nothing upstairs!
               People go dreaming with planning and scheming;
                   With thinking they make themselves drunk;
               But we've no responses to curdle our bonces,
                   'Cos never a thought have we thunk!
               True, one can succeed if one's born with the guts
                   And can sense any trouble that's brewing;
               But what is the use of our doing our nuts
                   When we haven't got nuts for the doing?
               Thinking unhinges what's under your fringes;
                   You wonder why nobody cares;
               You can worry yourself till you've bats in the bellf'.
                   We're all right! We've got nothing upstairs!

               We walk here and there, 'cos our feet are quite clever;
                   Our hands seem to get information.
               However, if anything preyed on our minds
                   It would very soon die of starvation!
               Though things go in one ear and out of the other
                   And ev'ryone meeting us swears,
               We keep all the while a most beautiful smile,
                   'Cos we know we've got nothing,
                   No, nothing, yes, nothing,
                   We know we've got nothing upstairs.

                              BLACKOUT

(Open traverse tabs.)

ACT ONE

SCENE FIVE - HOOD HALL, THE OLD HAUNTED HOUSE

(Full set.   A ruined gothic building set inside the Scene Three Forest
set, minus the wolf's house and the sloping bank cut-out piece on R.
wing.   All the pieces described are more or less separate to give the
effect of the shell of the building with glimpses of the forest in between
R. C. is the front doorway piece running up and down stage, with a
bell-pull attached to the D. S door post.   The door which is hinged U. S.
and opens onstage looks like heavy oak beams and is made in an upper
and lower half.   This is concealed when it is shut by a cross beam on
the onstage side attached to the lower half and overlapping top half so
that if top half is pulled open it operates both halves.   On the onstage
side of door there are a lock, two chains and three bolts on the lower
half and a chain and two bolts on top half.   On offstage facing side of
door is a knocker on top half.   In C. is a broken-off stone pillar, fairly
wide.   Between door and pillar on rostrum front are the two broken
sides of an arch with perhaps a tree glimpsed through them on back of
rostrum.   Running off R. along front of rostrum is a broken section of
stone wall so that it looks as if it leads off to another wing of the house.
L. C. of rostrum is a stone stairway with a rise of three or four steps,
backed by a section of ruined stone wall, with perhaps a window in it.
D. S. of rostrum in L. C. is a double stone archway, set at a slight
diagonal.   The upper archway has a door in it, which when opened
fully covers the lower archway.   D. L, opposite doorway, is a
revolving fireplace piece, which when turned round reveals a blank
stone wall.

Moonlight.   MUSIC 30.   SQUIRE puts head on D. R, looks around and
moves stealthily up to door.)

SQUIRE: I wonder whether there's anybody else here yet?   Apart
from the ghosts, of course, not that I believe in them.

(Sudden hoot of owl, SQUIRE jumps hastily round.)

Whassat?

(Hoot repeats.)

Oh, only an owl.   (Rattles door.)   Locked.   Now how am I going to
get in?   (Peers round below doorway.)   Ah!   (Walks round below
door to other side of it.)   I can let myself in.   (Unlocks lock,
release a chain, draws a bolt, then another, releases second chain and
draws a final bolt, and pulls open lower half of door.)   Walks round to
other side of door and walks into closed top half.)   Ow!   Curses!
(Walks back, draws both bolts and releases chain on top half, opens it,
walks round to other side of door.)   Well, now I can get in.   (Walks
through door, shuts both halves.)   I'd better lock up, I don't want just

anybody breezing in. (Locks lock, replaces the three chains and shoot. home the five bolts.) There. (Steps away. Door swings open after him. Worked by black line attached to top half onstage and pulled by SQUIRE.) Tcha! (Slams door shut testily.) Now I'll see if there's anyone through here. (Crosses U. L. Loud booming chime of midnight starts.) Ah, just midnight. (Exit SQUIRE through lower arch L. Enter HARDY and FOOLHARDY R each carrying a sheet.)

FOOLHARDY: Oo-er! It's creepy here. I don't like it.

HARDY: Neither do I. (Lifts knocker. Second chime of midnight starts, higher note.)

FOOLHARDY: Coo, one of those modern door chimes.

HARDY: Don't be silly, that's midnight chiming.

FOOLHARDY: What, again?

(SQUIRE enters U. L.)

SQUIRE: Mid-day already? How time flies. (Crossing to front doo Where have the others got to?

(Just as SQUIRE reaches door HARDY bangs hard on knocker pushing open both halves of door, to his surprise and hitting SQUIRE with it, wh falls upstage of it so that he is hidden by it while HARDY and FOOLHAF creep fearfully past it. FOOLHARDY shuts door.)

HARDY: It's all right. There's nothing here.

(SQUIRE sits up groaning.)

FOOLHARDY: W-w-what's that then?

HARDY: I-d-don't know, but don't let's stay to find out.

(They turn to run to door as SQUIRE rises before them.)

BOTH: Aah! Help!

SQUIRE: Lads! Stop squeaking like that!

HARDY: Oh, it's you, papa. Oh, papa, we don't like it here.

SQUIRE: Not like it? Ridiculous! Why, this is the old ancestral h of the Hood's. Many's the time I played here as a lad. It's all nonse people saying it's haunted. (Door U. L. opens, pushed by cane.)

Whassat! Ha-ha! The wind of course. (Crosses to door and flings i right back to cover lower arch.) See, there's nothing there.

(GREEN FLASH L, cymbal crash and door is flung back and DEMON is revealed in lower arch. Others screech and run off U. R on rostrum.)

DEMON: Come back! What meanth thith strange to-do?

SQUIRE: (in a very faltering voice) Is that a ghost?

DEMON: No, me.

SQUIRE: (coming on stage) Oh you. You're rather late.

DEMON: We thaid midnight.
'Tith but that now.

SQUIRE: Oh no, long past.

(Third chime of twelve starts, very high and quick.)

(Consults watch.)
I wonder if I'm slow or fast?
Well, anyway, the wolf is late.

DEMON: I've other worrith on my plate.
Too many folk are hurrying henth.

SQUIRE: Don't worry, we can jump that fence.
'Twas lest folk should I brought me boys
To drape in sheets as ghost decoys
And frighten off all prying eyes.

DEMON: Ah, thplendid. But perhapth 'twere withe
Letht fortune from our path thould thwerve,
To have thome goblinth in retherve.
Don't you agree?

SQUIRE: Why, yes, of course.

DEMON: Excuthe me, then, I'll reinforth.

(Exit DEMON L.)

SQUIRE: And I'll get the lads ready. I wish that blooming wolf would come, though. Exit U. R. MUSIC 31. Enter BAA and BAA-BAA D. L. and come to C.)

SHEEP: Baa! (They squat down and motion back to "come on".)

LUPE: (off R) Yes, all right, I'm coming. (LUPE enters R tied up in rope pinning his arms to his side from his shoulder to his wrists.) You can go off sheep, you know. I knew there'd be a catch in this rope idea. You do realise I'm supposed to be stealing you?

(The SHEEP nod.)

LUPE: Then perhaps you'd care to unravel me.

(The SHEEP nod eagerly.)

LUPE: Oh, no! If you feel like that about it, I'd rather stay tied up.

(But they have freed one end of the rope and now tug on it to set him spinning.)

Careful! Take it easy! Not so fast! (As soon as he is clear of the rope he spins off to L.and disappears through the fireplace which revolves to show the blank side. SHEEP look very astonished. Enter SQUIRE R. with HARDY and FOOLHARDY, all moving very warily until they see it is the sheep.)

SHEEP: Baa!

SQUIRE: Oh, it's only the sheep, lads. (To SHEEP.) But where's th wolf?

H & F: Wolf!

SQUIRE: Yes, wolf.

(SHEEP point with forehooves to wall. Loud glass crash off L.and cry of pain from LUPE. Fireplace revolves back and LUPE spins on with an inverted flower pot on his head, a tomato stuck in his mouth and a balloon painted to represent a marrow in his hands. He comes to rest between SQUIRE and his sons.)

HARDY: I thought you said a wolf, papa. This is a dog.

LUPE: (tries to speak and removes tomato from mouth and plonks marrow in SQUIRE'S arms) How dare you! I am a wolf.

FOOLHARDY: You're not.

LUPE: I am. (To SHEEP.) You two, aren't I a wolf?

(BAA-BAA mischieviously nudges BAA and they shake heads.)

LUPE: Ha! I knew I could rely on your support. (To HARDY and FOOLHARDY.) I am a wolf, I tell you.

HARDY &
FOOLHARDY: You're not.

LUPE: I am, I am, I am! And if anybody else says I'm not I'll - I'll squash this tomato in their face.

FOOLHARDY: (whispering) You're not a wolf.

LUPE: (is so exasperated he strikes forehead with hand, unfortunately the hand with the tomato in it. Practically in tears) I am a wolf.

SQUIRE: There, there, of course you are. But where have you been?

LUPE: In the greenhouse. And a darn silly place to leave a green-house it is.

SQUIRE: No, no, I meant, where have you been with the sheep? It's long after twelve.

LUPE: Is it?

SQUIRE: It certainly is, or I'm going cuckoo.

(Cuckoo clock strikes twelve.)

I'm going cuckoo. Now you can keep guard over the sheep through there. (Indicates U. L.)

LUPE: Theoretically, yes. In practice (Shrugs.)

(SHEEP run off through fireplace. LUPE runs after them)

Hey, come back! (LUPE AND SHEEP run on again through fireplace) See what I mean? (LUPE and SHEEP exit U. L. through Arch.)

SQUIRE: You two, go and put those sheets on and scare away anyone who comes nosing around by being ghosts.

FOOLHARDY: Suppose we run into some real ghosts?

SQUIRE: Then take the sheets off and scare 'em away by being your-selves.

HARDY &
FOOLHARDY: Yes, papa. (They exit U. R.)

SQUIRE: Ghosts - piffle! They're as likely to meet a ghost as this marrow is to go off pop. (Taps marrow with riding crop, which has a safety pin bound to the end of it and left open for this business. Marrow pops. He gulps.) Well, I never did believe in marrows, either. (Breaks into a run.) Help! (Exit through arch U. L. PRINCE & POPPET creep stealthily on D. R.)

PRINCE: Poppet, we're there.

POPPET: Yes, sir. And obviously the sheep aren't here so we'd better go again. (Turns to do so.)

PRINCE: (hauling him back) Poppet! First we must take a good look round.

POPPET: Certainly, sir. (Spins round once.) Done that. Ready to go now, sir?

PRINCE: Take a look up the stairs.

POPPET: Yes, sir. (Mounts stairs very shakily.) No, sir, there's noth- (Falls off end of stairs with a crash and a muffled cry.)

PRINCE: (running to foot of stairs) Poppet! Are you all right?

POPPET: (muffled) Yes, sir.

PRINCE: What did you find?

POPPET: (throwing open door in upper archway) A quick way down here.

PRINCE: Bad luck. Never mind, stay here while I explore along this wing here. (Exit U. R.)

POPPET: Stay here? On me tod? Waiting to be frightened by a lot of spooks? No likely. If you can't beat 'em, join 'em. And fortunately I just happened to bring a complete young haunter's outfit with me. (Takes out a sheet.)

(BO PEEP, wearing a large white tablecloth enters D. R. She does not seem to be able to see very well and blunders into upper half of doorway.

BO PEEP: (rubbing head) Oooooh!

POPPET: (is struck rigid. In fearful whisper) What was that? There only me here, and it wasn't me, so it must have been -

(Turns and sees BO PEEP just as she is coming through doorway.)

It was!

(Enter RED RIDING HOOD D. R. also covered with a tablecloth.)

Two of them! Aaaah!   (Runs U. L. and goes through upper arch.)

BO PEEP: What's that? Who's there? (Blunders into pillar.) Ow!

R. R. H: Bo Peep, are you all right.

BO PEEP: No, I can't see through my eyeholes.

R. R. H: (removing her own cloth) I'm not surprised.   After all, you havn't got eyes in the back of your head.

BO PEEP: (struggling out of her cloth) Well, they keep slipping.   Whew! I'm glad I'm not a real ghost.   It must get so stuffy.

R. R. H: Well, real ones don't have double damask dinner shrouds.

SQUIRE: (off U. L) Lads!   Lads!

R. R. H: Look out!

(They pull on their cloths.)

BO PEEP: I can't find my eyeholes again!

R. R. H: Ssh!   Don't talk, just moan.

(Enter SQUIRE U. L.   He moves down to R. of them.)

SQUIRE: Ah there you are, lads.   Hardy and ghoulhardy, eh? Ha ha ha ha.

R. R. H. &
BO PEEP: Whoo!   Whoo!

SQUIRE: Yes, all right, you needn't try to scare me.   I know you're not real.

(SQUIRE turns away from them as HARDY and FOOLHARDY enter U. R. draped in their sheets.)

Or you either.   Eh?   (Does a quick count.)   Four?   HELP!

(HARDY and FOOLHARDY very puzzled, scratch their heads as SQUIRE dashes U. L. to wrench back door now covering lower arch to reveal POPPET draped in his sheet.)

Aah!   Help!

(Slams door back to cover POPPET and dashes across to front door.)

Save me!   Save me! (Dashes through front door and off R.)

HARDY: I don't know what's the matter with him.

FOOLHARDY: Nor do -   (As they move down he sees the enrobed RED RIDING HOOD and BO PEEP.)   I do!

BOTH: AAH!

(They run round behind pillar chased by other two.   As they re-emerge POPPET pushes door away.   They shriek and push it back and run round below pillar and U. R.   POPPET pushes door more firmly to shut in Upper arch which surprises BO PEEP and RED RIDING HOOD as they come round.   They scream and run off D. L.   Just as HARDY & FOOL-HARDY have reached rostrum PRINCE appears U. R. on it barring their way with upraised axe.)

FLORIZEL: Poppet!

POPPET: (moving down) Yes, sir?

(HARDY and FOOLHARDY turn and run L. on rostrum and up stairs.   PRINCE chases after them.)

FLORIZEL: Quick, Poppet!

(Two crashes and two cries as HARDY and FOOLHARDY go off the end of the stairs.   PRINCE stops at foot of stairs.)

Where are you, Poppet?

POPPET: Here, sir. (Leans against fireplace and disappears through it.)

PRINCE: Where? (Looks around, jumps down and runs off through arch L.)

(Enter DAME TROT R.)

DAME: Ah, lovely quiet evening, isn't it? Well, here I am at Hood Hall. I expect you think I've forgotten why I came here.   But you're wrong. I wrote it down on a piece of paper, which I have (Looks in handbag.) - which I have - (Peeps down bosom.) - which I have - excuse me (Lifts skirt to look in knicker legs.) which I have quite forgotten to bring with me. Reminder, please.

(AUDIENCE shout. Plant grows, with leaf attached.)

Thank you. And there's my forget-me-not growing, even in Hood Hall. Of course, some people say it's haunted, but I don't believe it myself.

(As she crosses to plant HARDY and FOOLHARDY enter through lower archway U. L. see DAME, nudge each other and raise their arms, preparatory to haunting here.)

HARDY &
FOOLHARDY: WHOO! WHOO! WHOO!

DAME: Just hark at those owls. (Picks leaf, plant subsides.)

(HARDY and FOOLHARDY move down to her L.)

DAME: Oh, only a little leaf this time. Well, I shall have to remember all in one.(Eats.) And I have! I'm after the will and to find it I have to
look in the fireplace.

(Moves L. oblivious of HARDY and FOOLHARDY as she crosses in front
of them. They shrug and follow her.)

The only snag is - no fireplace.

(Turns L. looks U.S. POPPET bursts through fireplace turning it onstage.
At the sight of him HARDY and FOOLHARDY turn and run U.R. chased
by him. DAME turns D.S. and sees fireplace.)

DAME;   Oh. Marvellous how quickly they build these days. (Putting
head in fireplace.) Ah, here we are - the will! (Brings out small piece
of paper.) Or is it? (Reads.) "See under stairs". (Moves to do so.)

(BO PEEP and RED RIDING HOOD enter D.L. as PRINCE enters through
lower archway. Seeing them, he raises axe and gives chase. They run
shrieking off R, where HARDY and FOOLHARDY immediately bolt on
and run acroos to L. with the PRINCE following after them while DAME
searches under stairs.)

Listen to those bats squeaking.

(All run up stairs and off L, with suitable crashes and cries. DAME
finds a paper under stairs and moves down with it.)

Ah, this must be it. Or must it? (Reads.) "Look behind loose stone in
pillar". (Moves to pillar.)

(BO PEEP and RED RIDING HOOD enter as she moves round pillar clockwise, looking. When she is upstage of it door in upper arch L. is thrown
open and HARDY, FOOLHARDY and POPPET stream through. BO PEEP
and RED RIDING HOOD scream and, followed by the others, chase clockwise round pillar. DAME comes into sight again to below pillar, others
continuing D.S. and off D.L.)

What a lot of mice scurrying around. Oh, here's the loose stone.
Conveniently marked with an X - for a draw, of course. (Pulls it out and
finds small piece of paper.) This'll be it. Or will it? (Reads.) "Try
another forget-me-not leaf". Well, I don't think it'll have grown another
yet. (Plant grows with piece of paper attached which she takes and plant
subsides.) Ooh! it's grown a bit of paper instead. The will! Not the
will. (Reads.) "Go back to the place you first thought of". Well that's
the fireplace .

(All the others pour through fireplace and leave it at blank side running across to door just as SQUIRE is creeping in there, he immediately turr tail and all run off R.)

DAME: Ah, the dear little birds are starting to twitter their dawn chorus. I wonder if there's another clue here. (Turns over paper. Read "Look behind the firebrick marked with three crosses". Ah, a treble chance, of course. (Moves over to fireplace.) Eh? Well, I've heard of fires going out but this is ridiculous. (Looks away.)

(PRINCE rushes on through fireplace turning it round and stops just past DAME.)

PRINCE: Which way did they go?

DAME: Who dear? Haven't seen a soul. I'm looking for a fireplac myself.

PRINCE: Try that one.(Rushes to door and off R.)

DAME: But there isn 't - (Takes on it.) I must have my eyes tested. Now a firebrick with three crosses. (Puts head in fireplace.)

(Others run on D. R. to circle anti-clockwise round pillar. DAME finds will.)

I've found it! I've found the will'.'

(Chase stops. Ghosts fling off their diguises.)

ALL: What?

DAME: Goodness, where did everybody spring from?

R. R. H: What did you say you'd found, granny?

DAME: The will, dear, the will that proves you're the true heiress to the Hood fortunes!

SQUIRE: Curses! Then all is lost.

(MUSIC 32. Green flash L. and DEMON springs in through fireplace. Screams from others.)

DEMON: Courage Thquire, we'll yet win the day! (Snatches will fro DAME, who faints into POPPET'S arms.)

Goblinth! Fright thethe folk away!

(Some of CHORUS as GOBLINS leap on L. and chase the mortals off except PRINCE and SQUIRE, who stands rubbing his hands gleefully.)

DEMON: And thou! Theek not with me to fenth!

PRINCE: No, I'll not budge.

DEMON: Tho? (Casts spell over PRINCE who becomes transfixed.)
Bear him henthe. (GOBLINS take PRINCE off L.) And now thith will
we'll thwift dethtroy!

(WHITE FLASH R. Enter a very angry FAIRY R.)

FAIRY: How dare you extra help employ!
Still, that's a game that two can play. (Claps hands.)
Assistant Fairies! Haste this way!

(Remainder of CHORUS as FAIRIES enter R.)

Begone! You do the landscape spoil!

(Waves wand over SQUIRE who staggers back and disappears through
fireplace.)

And now fall to in battle royal!

(Balletic fight in which the forces of good and evil are urged on by their
respective leaders. The fortunes of war sway from one side to the other,
until the climax is reached when the DEMON is forced to yield the will to
the FAIRY and he and his GOBLINS are chased off L. Lighting starts to
change to a dawn effect.)

FAIRY: Enough! For lo the rising sun
Proclaims both light and right have won!

(OTHERS run on.)

OTHERS: We've won?

FAIRY: Yes! So your voices raise
And sing with me our hero's praise!
(Sings.) Turn again, Whittington,
                Thou worthy -
Oh no! Wrong ward. It's his turn next -
I've such a lot I get perplexed.
I meant, of course, Red Riding Hood,
Who'll now inherit all she should!
So joyfully I bid you say
A really loud hip-hip

ALL: - Hooray!

(MUSIC crescendo and CURTAIN. CURTAIN UP on same triumphant
picture, but with the addition of a fist shaking group of GOBLINS and
DEMON and SQUIRE D.L.) CURTAIN.

ACT   TWO

SCENE SIX - THE VILLAGE BEAUTY PARLOUR

(Fullset. On front of rostrum, five curtained cubicles numbered one to
five from R. to L. Wing L. with bell push and "PUSH FOR PERMANENT
WAVER" printed round it.   Wing R. with note "Our Speciality - MUD
PACKS 2/4½d a splodge". In front of this wing a counter running up and
down stage on a slight diagonal. On counter:- some papers, wig block
with wig on it, large book "EXERCISES", bowl marked "FINEST
SQUELCHY MUD". Just below counter a hat-stand. U. L. a hairdresser
chair with a hairdresser's sheet (waterproof) on it. A trolley on each side
of chair.

CHORUS boys and HARDY and FOOLHARDY discovered as Beauticians.

MUSIC 34 BEAUTY-FULL.)

ALL:	In our Beauty Parlour ev'ry pocket we can suit; We're the noted stockists of a thousand kinds of beaut -
HARDY & FOOLHARDY:	* We can give a wave, a pack, * Can lift your face or push it back.
ALL:	We can give you anything to make you what you're not!

(Enter DAME L.)

BOYS:	In our Beauty Parlour, etc.,
DAME:	I would like a -

(1st CHORUS GIRL dances in L.)

1st C.G:	* A slimming course, a slimming course, a slimming course.
HARDY & FOOLHARDY:	* We can give a wave, etc.,
BOYS:	We can give you anything, etc.,
DAME:	I would like a -

(2nd CHORUS GIRL dances in L.)

2nd C.G:	* A manicure, a manicure, a manicure.
1st C.G:	* A slimming course, etc.,

HARDY & FOOLHARDY:	* We can give a wave, etc.,
BOYS:	We can give you anything, etc.,
DAME:	I would like a -

(3rd CHORUS GIRL dances in L.)

3rd C.G:	* a beer shampoo, a beer shampoo, a beer shampoo.
2nd C.G:	* A manicure, etc.,
1st C.G:	* A slimming course, etc.,
HARDY & FOOLHARDY:	* We can give a wave, etc.,
BOYS:	We can give you anything, etc., In our Beauty Parlour, etc.,
DAME:	I would like a -

(BO PEEP dances in L.)

BO PEEP:	* a face massage, a face massage, a face massage.
3rd C.G:	* A beer shampoo, etc.,
2nd C.G:	* A manicure, etc.,
1st C.G:	* A slimming course, etc.,
HARDY & FOOLHARDY:	* We can give a wave, etc.,
BOYS:	We can give you anything, etc., In our Beauty Parlour, etc.,
DAME:	I would like a - I've forgotten what I would like now. Reminder, please!

(AUDIENCE shout. Plant comes up with leaf, which she picks a.. .ats.
Plant subsides.)

Yes.
I would like to have the lot, to have the lot, to have the lot.

BO PEEP:	* A face massage, etc.,

3rd C. G:	* A beer shampoo, etc.,
2nd C. G:	* A manicure, etc.,
1th C. G:	* A slimming course, etc.,
HARDY & FOOLHARDY:	* We can give a wave, etc.,
BOYS:	We can give you anything, etc.,

(*These lines should have a suitable action which is repeated each time. In last verse DAME tries to copy all the actions and ends up in an exhausted heap in the arms of HARDY and FOOLHARDY.)

DAME: Well, after all that I can't remember why I came here to be beautified.

BO PEEP: Oh, Dame Trot, because of the Squire's banquet to celebrate the Prince's arrival tonight.

4th CHORUS: And to welcome Red Riding Hood to her new estates.

DAME: Oh, yes, of course But I'm sure I don't remember seeing you two here before.

HARDY: We're the new head beauticians.

FOOLHARDY: Yes, papa's just taken over the shop.

(Enter SQUIRE R.)

SQUIRE: Exactly so, ladies. (Aside.) But little do they know I've only taken it over to put the prices up so high it'll pay for the banquet they've come to be beautified for.   Gad, what a devious mind I have! (To them.) Right, staff, to work and see what you can do to make all these lovely ladies even lovelier.

HARDY &
FOOLHARDY: Yes, papa. This way, ladies, this way.

(They and boy CHORUS shepherd out BO PEEP and girl CHORUS to R.)

SQUIRE: Aren't you staying for a beauty treatment, Dame Trot?

DAME: Yes, but I mustn't be too long. Red Riding Hood's asked me to deliver the will to a solicitor.

SQUIRE: Deliver the will to - ! You mean, you've got that will on you?

DAME: Yes, it's never leaving my side till it's safely delivered.
Well, not my side exactly, more - (Wriggles herself.) - well, not my
side.

SQUIRE: (leading her R.) I quite understand.   You go and get ready,
Dame Trot. I shall see you get a very special treatment.

(Exit DAME R.   SQUIRE rubs hands gleefully.)

Aha! The silly old faggot! I'll get my trusty lads to nab the will from her.
I can't do it myself because with the Prince arriving for the banquet tonight
I must nip back home and cook - yes, the royal rent books. (Going off D. R)
Hardy! Foolhardy!

(Exit. PRINCE'S head comes through curtains of cubicle No. four.)

PRINCE: Poppet!

(POPPET'S head through curtains of cubicle No. two.)

POPPET: Sir?

(They come onstage.)

PRINCE: You see, I knew we were right to keep an eye on the Squire.
Now, you stay here and make sure Dame Trot keeps the will. I'm going
to the Squire's house to steal a look at those rent books.

POPPET: Won't you find it a bit tricky getting in?

PRINCE: No. He's advertising for a flunky for the banquet tonight.
I'll go and take the job.

POPPET: But then how will you be yourself again at the banquet?

PRINCE: I shan't. I don't feel quite ready to be a Prince again yet.

POPPET: Well, who will be the Prince?

PRINCE: I rather thought -

SQUIRE: (off R) All right, lads. I leave it to you

PRINCE: Tell you later - quick, hide! I'm off.

(PRINCE hurries off L. POPPET runs out U. R.   Enter SQUIRE D. R.)

SQUIRE: That's arranged about the will - now for the rent books.

(LUPE pokes his head through curtains of cubicle No. three.)

LUPE: Psst!

SQUIRE: Is there a gas leak somewhere?

LUPE: Pssssst! Here!

SQUIRE: (turns up) Eh? What are you doing here?

LUPE: I want to know what to do with them.

SQUIRE: Do with who?

(BAA'S head comes through curtains of cubicle one and BAA-BAA'S through curtains of five.) Baa!

SQUIRE: Good gracious!

(LUPE and SHEEP come onstage.)

               Well, they're no use to me any more. Just lose them.

LUPE: But -

SQUIRE: Lose 'em.   (Exit L.)

LUPE: Oh, charming. There's gratitude for you. Well, in that case off you go, sheep, you're free.

SHEEP: (Shake heads and rub themselves affectionately against his leg)

LUPE: Here, nark it. I can't keep you. I'm a wolf. Well, if you won't leave me, I shall leave you.   (Moves L. and they follow.)
No, no! Shoo! Go away! (Turns and runs off.) Help!

SHEEP: (running after him) Baa!

(They exit L. Female scream off R.   POPPET runs on R.)

POPPET: How was I to know it was the changing room?

HARDY: (off R) Come on, FOOLHARDY.

(POPPET ducks down behind counter. HARDY and FOOLHARDY enter D.

FOOLHARDY: Well, I don't know how we're going to find this will.

HARDY: Papa said it was on her, so we'll have to try and make it drop out or something. Anyway, there's bound to be some way to find the will.

FOOLHARDY: Why?

HARDY: Because where there's a will there's a way.

          (Enter DAME TROT R. in a wrap over her underclothes and carrying a handbag.)

          Ah, good morning, Dame Trot.

DAME: Good morning.

HARDY: We'll start with some exercises.   Perhaps you'd take off your wrap.

DAME: Oh, I thought the treatment was just for my face.

HARDY: Oh no, we like to see if there's anything we can er - take away from the figure first.

FOOLHARDY: (helping her off with wrap)   Yes, and this might get in the will, I mean, the way.

          (As wrap comes off we see what is very obviously the will stuck in the waistband of her knickers at the front.)

H & F :   (pointing at it)   Ah!

          (POPPET looks up.   FOOLHARDY moves to hang wrap on hatstand, but looking back at DAME.   POPPET puts out a finger and FOOLHARDY unwittingly hangs it on that and returns to DAME.   POPPET puts wrap on and pulls his trousers up above his knees, then grabs wig from block on his knees, then grabs wig from block on counter and puts it on during the following.)

DAME: Oh dear, am I putting on weight round me tum?   What exercises do you suggest?

FOOLHARDY: Well, nothing too energetic or something might drop down. (Covertly indicates will to HARDY.)

DAME: I sincerely hope not.   I always use the very strongest elastic.

HARDY: I think we need something to get the head well back.   Let's try backward head jerks.

DAME: For me tum?

HARDY: Oh yes, you'll find it takes the mind off your stomach and things just disappear.

DAME: Very well. Would you put this with my wrap, then?
     (Gives HARDY handbag.)

HARDY: Certainly. (Passes it to FOOLHARDY. POPPET ducks
     down as FOOLHARDY turns and moves to hang up handbag. He is
     puzzled by the wrap's disappearance and puts handbag on counter and
     stands scratching his head with his back to the others. POPPET looks
     round top end of counter.) Now, head jerking - go!

     (DAME jerks her head back a little. HARDY puts a tentative hand out
     to snatch will, but hastily withdraws it as her head comes down again.)

     Not quite far enough back. Once again - go!

     (DAME jerks head further back. HARDY whips out will and quickly
     puts it behind his back as her head comes down again. POPPET
     creeps out from counter.)

     And once again - go!

     (DAME jerks head again.)

     (Aside, in whisper.) Oi! Take it!

     (POPPET takes will. FOOLHARDY, still looking at hat-stand puts out
     a hand to take will, POPPET grabs a paper from counter and puts that
     in his hand then nips back to hide behind counter. FOOLHARDY
     carefully puts paper away and turns back to others. POPPET comes
     up on R. side of counter, opens DAME'S handbag and puts will in.)

DAME: Couldn't we try something else now?

HARDY: Oh yes, anything you like now. Look up something in the
     exercise book, Foolhardy.

     (FOOLHARDY turns to counter to get book and sees POPPET.)

FOOLHARDY: Ooh, another customer.

HARDY: What can we do for you, madam?

POPPET: (keeps head averted to R. In falsetto) Oh, I just popped
     in for - er - (Looks round for inspiration. Sees Mud Pack notice.)
     for a mud pack.

     (Enter 5TH CHORUS.)

HARDY: Ah, Miss Jones. A mud pack for this lady.

2 - 6 - 67

5TH CHORUS: (taking mud pack bowl from counter) Oh, goody! I love
               giving mud packs. This way, madam. (Pushes a rather hestitant
               POPPET into cubicle 3.)

HARDY: Now, what other exercises have you found for Dame Trot?

(DAME tries to follow each direction as it is read out.)

FOOLHARDY: Er - "Place the hands on the hips, stand with the legs well
               apart - (Turns over.) - and with the feet together bend slowly forward
               to touch the toes".

DAME: What with?

HARDY: It does sound a bit tricky. (Looks at book.) Oh, Foolhardy,
               you've mixed up two exercises. We'd better get on to the beautifying.

(They bring down hairdressing chair to L.C. DAME sits. FOOLHARDY
puts the hairdresser's sheet round her. HARDY brings down R.trolley,
FOOLHARDY L.trolley.)

HARDY: We'll begin with the hair.   What sort of shampoo would you
               like?

DAME: A cream shampoo, please.

HARDY: No cream today, the milkman didn't leave any. How about
               a milk shampoo instead?

DAME: I've never tried that.

HARDY: Try one now then.   (Holds out the tumbler for FOOLHARDY
               who squeezes milk into it from the rubber glove.) How's that?

DAME: It smells a bit off.

HARDY: Ah, that's because it's a real poo and not just a sham one.

DAME: I think it might get my hair too wet.

HARDY: Not if you put this on.   (Gives her bath cap.)

FOOLHARDY: You could have a dry shampoo.

DAME: Not a milk one you mean?

FOOLHARDY: Yes, a dried milk one.   (Holds up tin of dried milk.)

DAME: I tell you what.   I'll have both.

H & F :   Righto.

(They pour the two things over her and go through the motions of shampooing.)

HARDY: Now, first rinse.   (Holds up watering can and sprinkles her with it.)

FOOLHARDY: Second rinse.   (Sloshes jug of water over her.)

HARDY: And that's the hair nice and clean.   Now a whiff or two of hot air from the hair dryer, please.

FOOLHARDY: Right.   (Takes up dryer and moves switch.)   Hot air.

(A jet of water squirts into DAME'S face.)

DAME: That felt rather more like cold water. I think a towel would be safer.

(HARDY towels her head and takes off her cap.)

HARDY: What hair style would you like? (Showing her wig on block.) I think this would suit you, but of course you'd need a perm.

DAME: Oh yes, I'd like to try that.

FOOLHARDY: I'll get the permanent waver then. (Pushes bell push on wing L. Permanent waving machine descends from flies in front of them. Its dangling clips make it look rather like a large spider.)

ALL 3:   Aaah!

DAME: Oh, I don't fancy that.   It might suddenly whisk up again and me with it.

HARDY: Oh, no fear of that.   Look.   (Clips wig onto permer.) See - safe as houses.

(Permanent waver rises quickly taking wig with it and leaving the bald wig block in HARDY'S hands.)

Yes.   Well.   Let's move onto the face.   You'd better put this on while we're applying the makeup. (Gives DAME headscarf which she ties round her head.)   Now, would you like a pancake?

DAME: No, I'm not very hungry, thanks.

HARDY: I meant a pancake make-up. (Picking up each tin as he mentions it.) Autumn Leaf Tan, Peach Bloom Blush or Rose Petal Pink. What have you got?

FOOLHARDY: (showing tin) Cherry Blossom black.

HARDY: Or should we make the most of the natural complexion with a mud pack?

FOOLHARDY: Oh, yes, let's.' (Picks up his bowl.)

DAME: Oh - er - do you think that's a good idea?

HARDY: Lovely! (Scoops up a handful and turns away contemplating the delights of plonking it in her face.)

FOOLHARDY: Gorgeous! (Does likewise.)

(DAME ponders a moment how to escape then scoops a little from each bowl and flicks the bits in HARDY and FOOLHARDY'S faces.)

BOTH: (turning in to each other) What are you playing at?
(They throw their respective handfuls at each other. As they reload, DAME ducks under their arms and runs up into cubicle four.)

HARDY: I'll teach you to chuck mud at me. Take -

(But FOOLHARDY lands his splodge, turns tail and runs off L. with HARDY chasing after him. Scream from 5TH CHORUS in cubicle three and she comes out backwards and turns to show a large splodge of mud pack on her face.)

5TH CHORUS: The beast! She fought back! (Runs off R. POPPET pokes head out through cubicle three curtains looking like a nigger minstrel.)

POPPET: (coming onstage) Why did I have to suggest a mud pack? She's made me look like a - (Picks up mirror from HARDY'S trolley.) well - Hallelujah!

(DAME and BO PEEP, with headscarves on, poke their heads through curtains of cubicles four and two respectively.)

DAME: Hallelujah, brother!

<u>MUSIC 35</u>. PRODUCTION NUMBER.

POPPET: Oh, sisters -

DAME & B.P.: Yeah, yeah.

POPPET: Say, sisters -

    (Enter some CHORUS.)

GIRLS: Yeah, yeah.

POPPET: Why don' you gather roun'?

    (Enter more CHORUS.)

GIRLS: A-men.

POPPET: While I sing to you,

    (Remainder of CHORUS enter.)

GIRLS: Yeah man!

POPPET: Yeah, I'll sing to you -

GIRLS: Glory Hallelujah!

POPPET: (spoken) I wish you'd stop interrupting!

                  All de beautiful songs I've foun',
                  Dose songs I've foun'.

(The number is then built up with suitable "standards" as desired.)

BLACKOUT

(Close traverse tabs.   Fly in Scene Seven Frontcloth.)

ACT TWO

SCENE SEVEN - OUTSIDE THE BEAUTY
PARLOUR

(Tabs to begin, frontcloth of street scene can be used later if desired.

MUSIC 36.   BAA-BAA and BAA run on L. looking for somebody and
skid to a halt R, BAA rather breathlessly.)

BAA-BAA: Baa?

BAA: (shrugging) Baa.

(LUPE puts his head on very cautiously L. and seeing the SHEEP,
immediately disappears.)

BAA-BAA: Baa! (Leaps up and runs L, beckoning for BAA to follow.)

BAA: (is not so quick off the mark, but sees obvious signs of
somebody running from L to R behind tabs and points it out to BAA-BAA.)
Baa!

BAA-BAA: (wheels round and points R) BAA!

(Both run off R.   Slight pause.   LUPE puts head on again L.   Tabs
open to reveal frontcloth if used.)

LUPE: Fooled 'em! (Enters.) Whew! It's all very well the
Squire saying "Lose 'em", but it's not been so easy.   After all the
trouble I went to stealing them for him, too.   Well, it's the last time
I do anyting for him.   No, I shall put my rearpaw down - and my
forepaw.   In fact, I'll put all four paws down.   He-he-he! I love a
joke, you know.   Ah well, back to my lovely little lair - and without
those sheep, at least.   (Turns to go R.)

BAA-BAA: (appearing in D. R. entrance) Baa!

LUPE: (turning to L) I spoke too soon.

BAA: (appearing in D. L. entrance) Baa!

LUPE: Much too soon.   Help! (Runs over catwalk and into
Auditorium.   HOUSE UP.)

BAA-BAA: (indicating to BAA they must give chase) Baa!

(LUPE runs along R (AUDIENCES') of auditorium and out through exit halfway along with the SHEEP following a little way behind. Enter DAME at equivalent entrance on opposite side of auditorium.)

DAME: Hullo, who's left the lights on here? (Making her way across transverse aisle and then down side aisle to catwalk.) Never mind, it gives me a chance to have a good look at you all. And I must say, you're not a bad bunch. By the way, you don't happen to have any sheep among you, do you? We're still looking for them, you see. I suppose that wolf's got them.

(LUPE looks on cautiously onstage L. and teeters on tip-paw across to R. and off.)

DAME: (going up steps on to stage) Still, I'm sure we're bound to find them sooner or later.

(BAA and BAA-BAA run on L. and stop, surprised, but quite pleased to see her.)

Well, what a coincidence! Oh, Bo Peep will be pleased.

LUPE: (popping head on R.) Not half so pleased as I am! (Disappears.)

DAME: It's particularly fortunate you've turned up now because you're just what I need to help me with - what was it to help me with? Remind me please.

(AUDIENCE shout. Plant comes up with leaf. She takes leaf and eats it. Plant subsides.)

Ah, of course. I was going to burst into song again. And I wanted you two because it's a song all about sheep. (Searching in handbag for it.) I wrote the words down on a handy piece of paper somewhere.

(SONG SHEET descends behind her. SHEEP point it out to her.)

Oh, good, I knew it couldn't be far away. Now, it goes like this.

MUSIC 37. "BAA-BAA-BAA".

The lambs in Spring,
They dance and sing -
    And very good singers they are! They are!
Though it sounds a strain
Ewe mutton complain.
    'Cos they sing three bleats to the Baa -
        Baa - Baa -
    They sing three bleats to the Baa.

I say, I've had an idea, I've written such big words I think we ought to
share them with all these people.

(SHEEP agree enthusiastically.)

DAME: By the way, can you sing? - Didn't quite hear you. Can
you? (To SHEEP.) They can. So let's have a bash. Thank you,
(Conductor's name. Stops AUDIENCE after a few bars.) I think we'd
better start again. I mean, I thought you were very good - the two of
you who did sing, that is - but I want you all to join in. Let's try
again, thank you, (Conductor's name. Sings a suitable number of
times with the AUDIENCE.) Well, that's come along very nicely.

(Enter POPPET L. SHEEP run and greet him very affectionately.)

POPPET: Dame Trot, you've found them! Bo Peep will be tickled
pink. You clever old thing you.

DAME: Yes, aren't I? We've been singing with all those people
down there. What do you think we ought to do now?

POPPET: Well, Bo Peep said Baa and Baa-Baa are very fond of
children. (Sheep agree.) So why not get some of them up here?

DAME: What a novel notion!

(HOUSE UP. Ad lib with children for song. POPPET, BAA and
BAA-BAA help the children up and then back again.)

Now, just one last time, altogether again.

(Fly song sheet as it is sung for last time, and close traverse tabs.
Fly out frontcloth. All exit waving, L.)

BLACKOUT

(Open traverse tabs.)

ACT TWO

SCENE EIGHT - THE SQUIRE'S BANQUET

(Full set.   Grand ballroom decor.   Wings L. and R.   On rostrum a set
of steps coming down from R. to C.   Steps down from rostrum in C.
A cut-out colonade of arches set along L. front of rostrum.   Bench U. R. C.
in front of rostrum.

BO PEEP and girl CHORUS discovered, girl CHORUS sitting on bench.
MUSIC 38.   "WALLFLOWERS".)

ALL:	Wallflowers, wallflowers, We're tired of being just wallflowers. We try to look cheerful as well as we can, But all that we want is a man.
BO PEEP:	We've dreamed of the handsomest men at the ball, But anything's better than nothing at all. To dance with a millionaire prince would be nice, But now we'll take anyone using "OLD SPICE".
ALL:	Wallflowers, wallflowers, Fashion-plate, passionate wallflowers. We try to look cheerful as well as we can, But all we want is a man.
BO PEEP:	We've done all the things the advertisements say, The right shade of lipstick, the right kind of spray; We've bought magazines to the end of our wealf, But now we'll be ordering "DO IT YOURSELF".
ALL:	Wallflowers, wallflowers, Unsated, frustrated wallflowers. We try to look cheerful as well as we can, But all that we want is a man, Is a man, But all that we want is a man.

(ALL go off.   Enter SQUIRE R.)

SQUIRE: Well, what a greedy gutted lot of guests, they've guzzled
all the wine already. I suppose I'll have to make some more now.
Curses!

(HARDY & FOOLHARDY look on L.)

HARDY: Psst, papa! We've got the will.

SQUIRE: Ah! Good lads! Good lads!

(They enter fully and give SQUIRE "will".)

I'll double your pocket money for this.

FOOLHARDY: But you don't give us any pocket money.

SQUIRE: Never mind, I'll still double it.   Ah!   (Opens out will.)
EH?   This isn't a will - it's a bill.   Clodpoles!   You've bungled things
again.   Just for that you can - you can - well, you can go and make
some more wine-cup for a start.   Go on!   (Bundles them off L.)   Look
at that - a bill, a silly stupid bill.   Unpaid at that.   (Tears it up.)   Now
what am I going to do?   That was my last chance.

(GREEN FLASH and DEMON leaps on.)

DEMON: Not quite!   There'th one latht card to play.
A winning trump though.

SQUIRE: Wat is't?   Say!

DEMON: Why, thinth dethtroy the will you can't
Dethtroy the girl.

SQUIRE: My sainted aunt!

DEMON: I thought you thaid the wath your coth?

SQUIRE: She is.   But that shocks me, it does.
No, 'tis a thing I could not do.

DEMON: Of courth.   'Twould not be withe for you
To theem connected with thuch deedth.
No, I know jutht who thith tathk needth.
He'th one whom we can eth'ly dupe,
A ready-made athathin -

SQUIRE: Lupe!

DEMON: Jutht tho.   Now litht unto my thcheme.
Thith crime a natural one mutht theem;
It thould take plathe within the wood.
Tho we mutht lure Red Riding Hood
Unto her grandma'th cottage, where -
Thinth we've made thure the Dame'th not there -
The wolf lieth lurking for the kill!

SQUIRE: How easily my mind you fill
With prospects of the purest joy!
My sons shall help me plot this ploy;
At once things under way I'll set.

(Exit L.)

DEMON: That Printh thome wind of thith might get,
But not if I can thcotch him firtht.
I'll raithe in him thuch raging thirtht
'Twill make the interfering pup
Drink far too deep the Thquire'th wine-cup!

(Exit DEMON L.   SQUIRE enters L.)

SQUIRE: Hardy! Foolhardy! Where are they?

(Enter CHORUS R and PRINCE L, as a rather grand flunkey carrying a staff, on rostrum.)

PRINCE: (bangs with staff) Sir False Hood, Ladies and Gentlemen, the guest of honour for this evening's banquet, the new heiress to the Hood estates - Red Riding Hood.

(BOYS and SQUIRE bow, GIRLS curtsey.   Enter RED RIDING HOOD down steps.)

SQUIRE: (aside) Curse her. (To her.) Greetings, my dear. I'm delighted to welcome you here to celebrate your new found fortunes.

R. R. H. : Thank you, Squire.   And I think it's very generous of you. I was afraid you'd be annoyed about that will granny found.

SQUIRE: Annoyed? Certainly not.   I'm - I'm - but let's not talk about the past, let us think only of the future.   And, of course, if you'd care to make your future doubly happy by marrying me -

(PRINCE steps between them banging with staff, ending with a bang on SQUIRE'S toe.)

OW!

PRINCE: So sorry, sir.   Sir False Hood, ladies and gentlemen, his Royal Highness, Prince Florizel.

(Fanfare.   Ladies curtsey, gentlemen bow.   Enter POPPET down steps. He has a false moustache, a long train and an overlarge crown.   He bestows a wink on the PRINCE in passing and then nods to the others. This jerks his crown over his eyes and he sets it right.   He stands waving a regally languid hand.)

POPPET: (to PRINCE out of the side of his mouth) What happens next

PRINCE: (out of side of his mouth) Tell them to rise.

POPPET: You may rise.

     (They do so.)

SQUIRE: Your Highness, this is a great honour.

     (POPPET nods graciously and tilts his crown again.   He sets it right
     and is about to move down from rostrum when he notices his train is
     still on stairs.   He hitches it off so that the end lands in front of him
     and he trips and falls as he steps forward, ending up sitting on rostrum
     trying to look as if that had been his intention.)

     Is your Highness all right?

POPPET: Of course.   I - er - I just felt a little tired after my journey.

SQUIRE: Did your Highness come by road?

POPPET: No, I - (Rising and tripping over train again) made the trip
     by train.   (Disgustedly whirls train over R. arm.)

SQUIRE: Your Highness, my I present my pretty little distant cousin?

     (RED RIDING HOOD curtseys.)

POPPET: She looks quite close to me.   (Extends R. hand.)   How do
     you - wait a minute   (Unravels hand.)   - do?

R. R. H. :   Your Highness.

SHEEP: (off L) BAA!   BAA!

SQUIRE: Was that sheep?

CHORUS: Sheep?

     (BO PEEP runs on L.)

BO PEEP: Sheep?

DAME: (off L) No wait, dears, not so fast!

     (MUSIC 39.   She is dragged on L. on rostrum by the SHEEP whom she
     holds on leashes.)

SHEEP: Baa!

ALL: The sheep!

(They leap off rostrum in C. to run to BO PEEP, jerking DAME after them. BAA-BAA goes upstage of POPPET and BAA D. S. so that DAME is pulled into POPPET, knocks him over and ends up sitting on him. Confused cries from all.)

DAME: And whom have I the honour of sitting on?

R. R. H.:   Granny, do get up, it's his Highness.

DAME: Dear me, and I've flattened him into a lowness. (Rising and helping him up.) I do hope I haven't made an unfortunate impression on you.

POPPET: Well, you certainly made an impression. (He moves R. and is jerked to the floor because DAME is standing on end of his train.)

DAME: It's just not your day is it? (Helps him up again.) Come and have a little sit down. I'll hold this up for you. Of course, what you really need is a shortie train.

(They exit R. and BO PEEP, SHEEP and CHORUS follow.)

SQUIRE: I'd better go and see that everything's all right. Excuse me, coz. (Hurries out R.)

R. R. H.:   I do hope granny didn't hurt him. Poor Prince Florizel.

PRINCE: What? Oh, my namesake, yes. What did you think of him?

R. R. H.:   Oh, he's rather a poppet, isn't he?

PRINCE: Er - yes.

R. R. H.:   Not at all what I expected.

PRINCE: Ah, but people aren't always quite what they seem, are they?

R. R. H.:   No. I thought you were a woodcutter.

PRINCE: Oh, I am. But I needed the extra money. I'm saving up, you see. In case, well, in case I get married, for instance.

R. R. H.:   Oh. You wouldn't think of marrying a girl for her money?

PRINCE: No, of course not.

R. R. H.:   Pity.

PRINCE: Would you think of marrying a man for his title - say a
            Prince?

R. R. H. : No, of course not.

PRINCE: Pity.

R. R. H. : I'd rather find myself someone to love.

PRINCE: I rather think I have.

R. R. H. : Me too.

PRINCE: Good.

    <u>MUSIC 40.</u>   "SOMEBODY"

BOTH: There must be
            Somebody whom I can have beside me,
            Somebody who'll always help and guide me,
            Somebody who'll be a lover and friend
                  Right up until the end.

            There must be
            Somebody whom I can sing my songs to,
            Somebody whom all my heart belongs to,
            Somebody who always will be true -
                  It could easily be you.
            It could easily,
                  Quite easily,
                  Most easily be you.

    (They exit L.   Enter POPPET R. with his train wound tightly round
himself.   Tries to extricate himself.)

POPPET: I should have known better than to try to twist in this.   I
            can't think why the Prince is shy of girls.   I find they're all much too
            busy being shy of a prince.   All I can get out of 'em is "Yes, your
            Highness", "No, your Highness", "Three bags full, your Highness",
            even Bo Peep, worse luck.   I think I'll dump this clobber and be myself
            for a bit.   (Goes behind an arch on rostrum.   Enter SQUIRE L. carrying
            a goblet and HARDY with two small gilt chairs and FOOLHARDY with a
            little table.)

SQUIRE: Come on, lads.   Put those down there.   (They put the chairs
            and table down L. C.)   Now listen, when I bring that old haybag Dame Trot
            here you'll have prepared this drink for her with the knock-out drops.
            Right? (Puts goblet down on table.   POPPET puts head out to listen).

H & F: Right.

SQUIRE: And as soon as she passes out you take her and dump her in the woods.

FOOLHARDY: Couldn't we dump her in her cottage?

SQUIRE: No, you blithering idiot! The whole point is that when I tell Red Riding Hood her granny's been taken ill and she goes to the cottage to see her -

HARDY: She'll have to come back again because her granny's not there.

SQUIRE: NO. She doesn't find her granny in the cottage.

FOOLHARDY: She finds her down in the dumps.

SQUIRE: Will you be quiet? She finds the wolf waiting to gobble her up.

H & F : Coo!

HARDY: Won't that make her a bit cross?

SQUIRE: Ah, lads, believe me I'm only doing this for your good. Now I'll go and find Dame Trot and chat her up a bit. You prepare the drink Oh, and get a basket of goodies ready for me to give Red Riding Hood.

HARDY: Yes, papa.

(Exit SQUIRE R. and HARDY and FOOLHARDY L. POPPET emerges.)

POPPET: Cor! I must tell his Highness at once. (Trips over train.) Oh, blow! Ah, I know. (Pulls end of train through his legs and throws it over his shoulder.) That's better. Your Highness, I mean, Flunkey Flunkey! (Exit POPPET R. Enter HARDY and FOOLHARDY L, carrying a vast bottle labelled "M. FINN'S ORIGINAL KNOCK-OUT-DROPS".)

HARDY: Papa always gets things in the large economy size.

(FOOLHARDY holds glass while HARDY pours out drops.)

FOOLHARDY: He'd better get some more then, we've run out.

HARDY: Well, anyway there's just enough. Let's get the basket of goodies ready.

(They put bottle down. Exit L. MUSIC 41. Enter DEMON U. L. on rostrum, holding bowl of wine-cup and moving to bench.)

DEMON: Aha! I'll plathe thith on the bench
And lure the Printhe his thirtht to quench!

(Enter PRINCE D. L.)

PRINCE: I wish that I this thirst could slake.

(DEMON smiles delightedly and beckons PRINCE.)

Well, no one's here, so this I'll take.

(DEMON is rather taken aback as PRINCE drinks. MUSIC ting. He crosses R. yawning.)

I think I must have drunk too deep,
For now I crave not drink but sleep.

(Exit D. R. DEMON moves down.)

DEMON: Curtht be! My plan hath gone amith!
Now I thall have - But, thtay! What'th thith?

(Examines label on bottle.)

Not quite how I'd thought to play the game,
But never mind, the end'th the thame!

(Exit D. L. HARDY and FOOLHARDY re-enter L.)

HARDY: Goodies done. Drink done. (Sees goblet is empty.)
Here - where's it gone?

FOOLHARDY: Coo! It must have evaporated.

HARDY: But that was the last of the drops. There's only the bottle left - what's the use of - ? Still, I don't know. This 'ud knock her out if it dropped on her.

FOOLHARDY: Yes, but it's not likely to, is it?

HARDY: Well, it might, if it were sort of - helped a bit.

SQUIRE: (off R) Come along, Dame Trot.

HARDY: Here they come! Quick, fill this up and we'll pretend nothing's happened.

(Exit FOOLHARDY L with goblet. Enter SQUIRE and DAME TROT R. HARDY hides bottle behind back.)

SQUIRE: Come on, you devastating little devil, tickle your tonsils
        with a tiny tot of - (To HARDY.)   Where is it?

HARDY: Just coming, papa.

SQUIRE: Ah, won't be a moment, my priceless pearl.   Do sit down.

DAME: Thank you.   (As she crosses to do so SQUIRE lifts chair
        up to dust it gallantly with his hanky and she lands on floor.)

SQUIRE: Oh, I do beg your pardon.   Have you hurt your little self?

DAME: Well, I've hurt my little something.

        (SQUIRE helps her up.   Enter FOOLHARDY with goblet L.)

SQUIRE: Ah, here's your drink.

        (HARDY keeps raising and then lowering bottle during following.)

DAME: (takes drink)   Thank you.   Oh, aren't you having any?

SQUIRE: Not just now.

DAME: Well, have a sip of this.   (Handing it to him.)

SQUIRE: NO!   (Pushes it back.)   I wouldn't dream of depriving those
        cherry lips of a single drop.

DAME: Oh, very well, then.   (Drinks.)

SQUIRE: Ah!

        (Starts to put goblet down and SQUIRE notices she has not finished it.
        Pushes it back to her mouth.)

        Naughty, naughty, no heel taps.   There.

        (HARDY swings bottle back over his head and hits FOOLHARDY with it.

FOOLHARDY: Ow!   (Snatches it from him.)   Let me do it.

SQUIRE: Feeling a little tired?

DAME: Not a bit.

FOOLHARDY: You will in a minute.   (Swings bottle to R and hits HARDY
        chest.)

HARDY: Ouf! We'd better do it together.

SQUIRE: (aside) Very slow acting. I'd better try and tire her out a bit. (To her.) Come, let us dance. (Pulls her to her feet as HARDY and FOOLHARDY crash the bottle down to fall on the chair from which she has risen.)

DAME: Oh yes, I love dancing. I was always a great dancer as a girl.

SQUIRE: Ah, if only I had known you as a girl. How we would have danced together then.

      MUSIC 42. "DANCING TIME".

BOTH: They were grand old days at the Palais de Dance
When we were in our prime;
And the songs that were sung when the world was young,
Have stood the test of time.
Our joy was not just the old gavotte
Or the minuet so gentle;
But the lancers fleet and the polka's beat
And the waltz all sentimental.

(They waltz to "Blue Danube".)

       We remember the days of the Charlston craze
And the warm, exotic tango
And the foxtrot blue, and the quickstep too
That made your corsets bang-o.
But we're not afraid we'll get old and staid
Though the years are fast advancing;
We will twist and jive while we're still alive
To enjoy this modern dancing.

(They dance whatever is the current rage.)

(During Number HARDY and FOOLHARDY try from time to time to hit DAME but keep missing as she always moves when they are about to deliver the blow. Finally the DAME and SQUIRE change places so that they hit him and knock him down and she goes spinning off on her own. They look down at him and then at the bottle, which they are holding out in front of themselves. DAME trips in her dance and crashes headlong into bottle knocking herself out. HARDY and FOOLHARDY shake hands in self-congratulation and bow to AUDIENCE as number ends. SQUIRE sits up rubbing head.)

SQUIRE: Ooh, what happened?

HARDY: There was a little trouble with the knock out drops, papa. But it's all right now.

SQUIRE: Right. Well, go and dump her then. (MUSIC 43.) And quickly, they're all coming dancing in here. (Rises.)

HARDY: Yes, papa.

(FOOLHARDY takes the bottle off and HARDY exits dragging DAME. CHORUS dance in.)

SQUIRE: Now to deal with Red Riding Hood.

FOOLHARDY: (putting head on L.) Psst, papa. The basket of goodies.

SQUIRE: Oh, goody.

(FOOLHARDY gives basket to SQUIRE and disappears. Enter RED RIDING HOOD R.)

SQUIRE: Ah, Red Riding Hood. I have bad news for you, I'm afraid. Your poor old grandmother is ill.

R.R.H.:   Granny ill?

(Dancers stop, music dies, general buzz of excited comment.)

SQUIRE: Yes, I've had her taken back to her cottage.

R.R.H.:   I must go and see her at once.

SQUIRE: Of course, my child. And here's a basket of goodies for you to take her. She seemed very ill indeed.

R.R.H.:   Then I must hurry. Thank you Squire. Goodbye. (She hurries out up stairs. General goodbyes and sympathetic remarks.)

SQUIRE: Goodbye, my dear. Ladies and gentlemen, I'm sure Red Riding Hood would not wish to spoil your enjoyment. Pray, carry on with the dance.

(MUSIC 44. They recommence dancing.)

Aha! Soon, soon she'll be at the mercy of the wolf and then - the wolf! We haven't arranged for him to be at the cottage! Where's that Demon, there's not a moment to lose! (Hurries out L. Enter POPPET and BO PEEP R.supporting a very drowsy PRINCE. POPPET is now without crown, cloak and moustache.)

POPPET: Come on, sir, there's not a moment to lose.

PRINCE: But I'm so tired, so tired.

BO PEEP: And I still don't understand Poppet, I thought that you -

POPPET: Never mind that now.   He's obviously drugged - we must
     keep him walking.   It's our only chance.

BO PEEP: Only chance to what?

POPPET: Our only chance to save Red Riding Hood!

(MUSIC crescendo.   The dancers swirl round them as they move up to
steps urging PRINCE to "wake-up!".

BLACKOUT

Traverse tabs close.   Fly in frontcloth.)

ACT TWO

SCENE NINE - IN THE WOODS

(Frontcloth or Tabs. If cloth is used, a woodland scene. Scene two cloth could be repeated. Open traverse tabs during scene as soon as frontcloth is in.

MUSIC 45. Enter HARDY and FOOLHARDY L. carrying DAME TROT on a stretcher. FOOLHARDY is walking backwards.)

FOOLHARDY: Oi! How much farther are we going?

HARDY: I don't know. Papa just said to dump her in the forest.

FOOLHARDY: Well, do we have to walk backwards to do it?

HARDY: I'm not walking backwards.

FOOLHARDY: I am.

HARDY: Are you? Let's turn round then.

(They lower the D. S. pole and raise the U. S. one - so that DAME tips out - and turn U. S. and inwards, stepping over the original D. S. pole so that they are now facing each other.)

FOOLHARDY: Ah, that's better. It's lighter this way too.

(They exit L. DAME sits up.)

DAME: Ooh! Where am I and why? (Looks round.) In the woods. But my mother said I never should. The last thing I remember is being at the Squire's Banquet. Well, the sooner I get home, the better. (Rising.) Ooh, me bonce - I beg your pardon, me nut. I must be suffering from a nasty overhang, or whatever it's called. How dreadful at my time of life. Well, I shall never touch alcohol again. In future I'll stick to Guinness. (Exit R. Enter SQUIRE and DEMON L. carrying LUPE by his elbows. They stop in C.)

LUPE: Hey, leggo, put me down, I say;
I've told you, I don't want to play.

SQUIRE: Oh, come, it's such a simple task.

DEMON: To have a meal ith all we athk.

SQUIRE: Our only thought is for your good.

BOTH: Just gobble up Red Riding Hood!

LUPE: No! I've gone right off eating meat.

    (Tries to go, they pull him back.)

BOTH: Well, we've no wish your head to beat -

    (They clonk him.)

DEMON: Your arm to twitht -

    (Twists it.)

SQUIRE: Your tail to tweak -

    (Pulls it.)

                  But if you don't -

DEMON: Why, we might thneak -

BOTH: And have you hung for stealing sheep!

LUPE: (bursts into tears)
                You cads!

SQUIRE: There, there!

DEMON: No need to weep.
                Jutht thay you will.

LUPE: All right.

BOTH: (slapping him on back)   Well done!

SQUIRE: You'll find the plan's a simple one
                For I've ensur'd the Dame's not there.
                But to her cottage let's repair,
                The rest I'll tell you on the way.

    (Exit SQUIRE and LUPE L.)

DEMON: And I'll Red Riding Hood delay.
                Thome woodland flowerth there I'll grow.

    (<u>MUSIC 46</u>. Indicates R, makes magic pass. BLACKOUT. A little bank with a cluster of woodland flowers is put on R. Also a plant with dock leaves attached to a thin batten of wood which goes underneath frontcloth so that it can be made to slide along from behind. LIGHTS UP.)

2 - 9 - 88

But when the thtoops to pick them, though,
The'll find that midtht the harmleth petalth
There lurk thome nathty thtinging nettlth!
The dock leavth purpoth thoon you'll thee.
Now, I mutht make mythelf to be
Invithible unto her eyth.

(Looks off L.)

And quickly too for henth the hieth.'

(Makes pass over himself.   MUSIC ting.   Enter RED RIDING HOOD L.

R. R. H. :   Poor Granny being taken so,
How can I cheer her? Ah, I know,
I'll pick her those few flowers there.

DEMON: (nodding as she bends to do so)
Aha!   The'th falling for my thnare!

R. R. H. :   (clasping hand in pain)
Ooh!   There are nettles growing here.
I hope some dock leaves too are near.

(DEMON points to dock leaves.   As she puts her hand out to pick one
DEMON beckons with his finger and the dock leaves slide along to L.
MUSIC whizz.)

How odd.

(Tries again DEMON beckons and they move.   MUSIC whizz.)

They slide from place to place,
In fact, a plant you have to chase.

(DEMON goes off L. beckoning, plant follows and RED RIDING HOOD.
MUSIC 47.   Enter FAIRY R.)

FAIRY: You'll really think I've been remiss
But I've been waiting for a kiss -
For just about one hundred years.
'Twas not, of course, for me, my dears,
But my ward, the Sleeping Beauty;
To whom it was my bounden duty
To see she didn't oversleep.
Now what's been happ'ning here. I'll peep.

(Puts lorgnettes to eyes.)

Dear me, things take a nasty trend,
Red Riding Hood will meet her end
Unless she's saved by Florizel.
But see what that poor lad's befell -
He's half asleep upon his feet.

(Hurries to catwalk and through Auditorium.   HOUSE UP.)

Well, I know how that trick to beat.
He needs some coffee, black as tar.
I'll nip and get some from the bar.

(Exit at back of Auditorium.   HOUSE OUT.   Enter POPPET and BO
PEEP supporting the PRINCE L.   They walk him to and fro.)

BO PEEP: Oh, Poppet, I'm exhausted!

PRINCE: (very drowsily)   So am I, Poppet, so am I.

POPPET: I know, but we must keep walking, sir.   Thank goodness
we didn't bring your sheep.

BO PEEP: Why?

POPPET: He might have started to count them, then we'd really be
done for.   But he's getting better now.   Aren't you, sir?   (No
response.   Shakes him.)   Sir!   You're more awake, aren't you sir?

PRINCE: Wh- what?

POPPET: MORE AWAKE?

PRINCE: Oh.   Yes.   Awfully.   Awfully awake.   (His head drops
forward with a slight snore.   They drag him off R.   HOUSE UP.
Enter FAIRY at back of Auditorium with cup of coffee.   She hurries
to catwalk and onstage.   HOUSE OUT when she is back.)

FAIRY: There, coffee steaming hot and black,
This will bring his senses back.
And just to make sure all goes well
I'll lace it with a potent spell.

(Waving wand over cup.   MUSIC 48.   Shimmer LIGHTS.)

Mix and stir and stir and mix!
Like unto a magic fix
Make his lassitude depart
Swifter than the purplest heart!

(LIGHTS and MUSIC finish.)

> And ere again he this way comes,
> Supported by his loyal chums,
> Since some find Fairies risible
> I'll make myself invisible.

(Touches self with wand.   MUSIC ting.)

> Ouch!

(Others re-enter R.)

POPPET: That's the way, sir, keep it up.

BO PEEP: Of course, he really needs a cup
> Of coffee strong and sweet and hot.

POPPET: I know, but strange to say it's not
> A thing to find in a woodland nook.

(FAIRY pushes cup in front of him.)

> Well, what a turn up for the book!

(Looks round.)

> Not a sign of a nearby cafe.
> I wonder - do you think it's safe?

BO PEEP: If I were you, I'd risk a sip.

(POPPET gives PRINCE a sip.)

POPPET: Hm.   Doesn't seem to have much zip.

(PRINCE suddenly comes to life, rushes to L. and over catwalk into auditorium.   HOUSE UP.)

PRINCE: Come! Quickly, Poppet, through the wood
> And help me save Red Riding Hood!   stay at bac

(PRINCE exits at AUDIENCE'S L. of Auditorium at side.   BO PEEP and POPPET hasten after him.)

POPPET: Hey! Not so fast, sir! Wait! Come back!

BO PEEP: You'll lose yourself along that track!

(They follow through same exit.   FAIRY runs after them.)

FAIRY: I must quickly right this wrong,
                That spell was p'raps a mite too strong.
                Still, rather good for just one taste.

(PRINCE enters at R. back of auditorium.)

PRINCE: Hurry, Poppet!   We must make haste!

(Exit at R. side.   FAIRY turns and runs after him.   POPPET and BO
PEEP run on at L back.)

POPPET: I think he's here!   No, my mistake!

(They turn and run back the same way.   PRINCE enters at R. again
and hurries across transverse aisle to L.)

PRINCE: Hurry, Poppet, for heavens sake!   (Goes out L.   FAIRY
        runs on R.)

FAIRY: Well, even if it's round the bend,
                I vow he'll get there in the end!

(Disappears through L. exit.   HOUSE OUT.   Onstage - MUSIC whizz
and enter dock leaves L. and RED RIDING HOOD chasing them to R.
DEMON follows her on.)

R. R. H. :   I think these leaves grow more perverse.
                Now they're going in reverse!

(DEMON puts up hand, they stop.   R. R. H. picks one and rubs hand
with it.   Close traverse tabs.   Fly cloth.)

                I've heard of creepers ere today,
                But not of plants that run away.
                But still at least they've stopp'd the pain,
                Now I must hurry on again.

(Exit R.   MUSIC 49.)

DEMON: That'th it, thweet child, don't thtop or wait,
                But go full thwift to meet your fate!

(Laughs fiendishly.)

BLACKOUT

(Open traverse tabs.)

2 - 10 - 92

ACT TWO

SCENE TEN - DAME TROT'S COTTAGE

(Full set. Cottage cut-out ground-row at front of rostrum. Cottage
wing R. with door opening onstage. Booked cottage wing L, set with
apex of "L" onstage. In section running straight up and down stage a
practical door hinged upstage and opening onstage. In section running
straight across and offstage a large practical casement window, hinged
L. and opening onstage through which we can see people arriving at the
door. In front of window a small table with a pot plant and a shopping
basket on it. R. C. a bed with a cover over it. Red cloak on foot of
bed. Warming pan in bed and a club beneath the pillow. L. of bed a
chair with a nightdress and mob cap on it. R. of bed a table with a
candlestick and prop candle in it; lines attached to candlestick going
offstage. Small batten on R. end of table to prevent candlestick going
off.

Candle-light goes on as lights go up to discover DAME TROT with her
dress half off. She hastily and modestly pulls it up again.)

DAME: Ooh! Who turned my candle on? It's such a powerful
candle too. isn't it? I was just getting undressed - with all you lot
sitting out there I thought I'd better do it in the dark. Well, I'll nip
and do it in the kitchen instead. (Picking up nightdress from chair.)
I'll take me nightie with me. Oh no, I put one to warm by the kitchen
fire. (Leaves nightie and cap on chair. (Crossing to R. of door.)
Well, there's nothing worse than going from a warm undie into a cold
nightie, is there? (Exit R. Momentary clatter of kettle, cup and
saucer and she returns almost immediately in a nightie and mob cap
holding a cup of tea.) I made myself a cuppa while I was out there.
(Drinks.) Lovely. (Puts cup down on table (Clear of candlestick
working lines), and picks up cloak from foot of bed.) Oh, I keep
forgetting to give Red Riding Hood this old cloak she left here. I know
I'll put it in me shopping basket. (Crosses to table below window and
puts cloak in basket, then returns to bed.) Now bed. (Pulls back bed
cover to reveal a large knot in the top blanket.) Hm, what was that I
had to remember? Ah well, can't have been important. (Gets into
bed and leaps out again clutching behind.) OW! That's what I had to
remember. (Takes out warming pan and puts it off R. Starts to get
into bed again and notices she still has her boots on.) Silly me - I've
forgotten to polish them. In we get. (Starts to lie down.) Oh, the
light. (Blows candle, nothing happens, tries again, still nothing.
Prepares to take a mighty breath, candlestick whisks to other end of
the table. MUSIC whizz.) Coward. Now come back here, you
naughty thing. Come on.

(Candle travels back very slowly.)

Come on. That's it. I promise I won't hurt you. (Gives a very
little puff. Candle goes out. DIM LIGHTS.) That's a good little
candle. (Pats it. LIGHTS UP and Candle on.) Ow! Oh well, I'll
just turn you down. (Bends candle over. DIM LIGHTS PARTIALLY.
She lies back with a thump.) OUCH! (Takes a large club from under
pillow.) Nearly laid meself out on me own night security. (Puts club
on table.) I say, though, what about the Squire courting me, eh? Ah,
that's one thing I do remember, me courting days. Yes -

MUSIC 50. "WHEN I WAS YOUNG".

>When I was young,
>   Well - thirty-three,
>A fine young man came a-courting me.
>He said, "Let us marry", and I said, "Yes",
>   So we liv'd together in happiness.
>
>When I was young,
>   Well, thirty-four,
>We had a babe - just the one, no more.
>A dear little girl, whom we call'd Bess;
>   So three liv'd together in happiness.
>
>When I was older,
>   Well - a year or so,
>My fine young man to the war had to go.
>He never came back and oh my distress;
>   I thought I'd ne'er again know happiness.
>
>Now I am old,
>   Well - never mind,
>In grandmotherhood my joy I find,
>And each day I live is a day that I bless
>   So I live by myself in happiness.

(Gently blows out candle. DIM LIGHTS. She lies down then puts her
head up a moment.)

>Nighty-night.

(Slight pause with a snore or two from DAME. MUSIC 51. LUPE
comes into sight at window.)

LUPE: (whispering) How shall I get in?

SQUIRE: (off L, whispering) Try the window - and hurry. Red
Riding Hood'll be here at any minute. (Also coming into view.)
Anyway, what are we whispering for? The old girl's not here. Hardy
and Foolhardy dealt with her.

(LUPE opens window and knocks over flower pot.)

DAME: (sits up) What's that? Who's there?

SQUIRE: Curses! They've bungled!

DAME: Where's me matches?

LUPE: Well, that's that then. (Starts to shut window. SQUIRE stops him.)

SQUIRE: No! Here's a bit of luck - a red cloak and a basket. (Take them from table in front of window.) Put it on.

LUPE: What, the basket?

SQUIRE: No, the cloak. (Helps LUPE into it.) Now you can say you've brought your granny a basket of goodies because you hear she wasn't well.

LUPE: But there's nothing wrong with my granny.

SQUIRE: Fool, I mean, pretend you're Red Riding Hood so you can get in and overpower her. (Disappears.)

DAME: Who is it out there?

LUPE: Oh - er - (Clears throat and assumes a piping voice.) Little Red Rooding Hide.

DAME: What?

LUPE: I mean - Little Rood Hiding Head.

SQUIRE: (bellowing) Little Red Riding Hood.

LUPE: (bellowing) Little Red - (Quietly.) Little Red Riding Hood

DAME: Well, come in, dear.

LUPE: I can't seem to get in, Granny. How does the door open?

DAME: The usual way, dear. Pull the bobbin and the latch will fly up.

(LUPE does so and enters.)

You're out very late aren't you, my love?

LUPE: Well, I heard you were ill, so I brought a basket full of
grannies for my dear old goody. I mean, a granny full of goodies for
my dear old basket.

DAME: Dear, dear, you don't sound yourself at all.   I wish I could
find me matches so I could take a good look at you.   (Finds them.)
Ah, here they are.   (Lights match and puts it to candle which slides
away to R. MUSIC whizz.   Moves match to candle, it moves R. again
MUSIC whizz.) It must have a floating wick.   (Puts match behind
candle so that it moves into flame and lights. MUSIC whizz. LIGHTS
UP.)   Fooled it.   Now then - (Turns.) Aaahh!

(LUPE leaps at her with a growl, but she moves upstage of him and
grabs club and hits him with it as he lands on bed.)

LUPE: (crawling off bed and running D. R.with DAME hitting him)
Ow! Help! Help! I surrender! (Trips and falls by forget-me-not
plant.)

DAME: So I should think you naughty - er, naughty - Oh, what are
you? Pussy-cat? No, dachshund - budgerigar. Oh, it's no good.
Reminder, please!

(AUDIENCE shout.   Plant grows with leaf attached.)

Thank you.   (Takes leaf.   Plant subsides.) Very fashionable these
house plants.   (Eats.) Ah yes, you're a naughty wolf - a wolf! Ooooh.
(Staggers back and faints very carefully on bed.)

SQUIRE: (looking round door L) What's going on? (Coming in.)
Ah, good, you've done it.

LUPE: Er - yes.

SQUIRE: Don't just lie there, then - give me a hand with her into the
kitchen before she recovers.   (As they take DAME off R.)   I'll tie her
up and you find another nightie to disguise yourself in.

(LUPE returns taking off cloak and throwing it under bed.   He sees
nightdress on chair and starts to put it on putting legs through sleeves.)

LUPE: All this dressing up.   Ridiculous.   How do you get into
these things?

(SQUIRE returns.)

And when you've got into 'em, how do you keep 'em up?

SQUIRE: Don't be silly.   You don't wear it that way up.

LUPE: You mean, I have to stand on my head?

SQUIRE: No, no, get your arms where your legs are.

LUPE: (trying to get arms into sleeves as well) Be a bit uncomfortable won't it?

SQUIRE: Take it off and start again. (Helps LUPE into nightdress.) That's it. Now, this on your barnet - (Puts mob cap from chain on LUPE'S head.) And you look lovely.

LUPE: Oh, you're only just saying that. White's not really my colour at all.

SQUIRE: Never mind, get into the bed and wait for Red Riding Hood. I'm nipping off before she turns up. (Moves to door and RED RIDING HOOD appears in window and knocks on door, which startles them. LUPE stumbles and falls just as he is getting into bed and SQUIRE jumps away from door.)

R.R.H.: Granny!

SQUIRE: (hoarse whisper) Too late! I'll hide under the bed! (Dives under bed.)

R.R.H.: (knocks) Granny, are you there? Can I come in?

LUPE: (assuming a granny voice) Oh yes, my dear. I'm bed and quite indecent. I mean, I'm in bed and quite decent. Just pull the - er - (Leaning over R.of bed to SQUIRE.) Pull the what was it?

SQUIRE: (putting head out R. Whispering) Pull the bob-

LUPE: That's it. (Calling.) Pull the bob out-

SQUIRE: In.

LUPE: In. And the latch will fall off.

SQUIRE: Fly up!

LUPE: Wait a minute, she's not in yet.

SQUIRE: The latch will fly up!

LUPE: Sorry. (Calling.) The latch will fly up.

R.R.H.: (opens door and enters. Laughing) I know that, granny, after all these years.

LUPE: So much for my little touch of originality.

R. R. H.:   I think you must have caught a nasty cold.   Your voice is very hoarse.

LUPE: (aside) Just so long as it's not wolf.

R. R. H.:   I suppose that's why you've got those fur mittens on in bed.

      (LUPE hides forepaws under blankets.)

      In fact, you don't look right at all.

LUPE: (aside) Well, I tried my best.

R. R. H.:   For one thing, what big eyes you've got, Granny.

LUPE: (aside to SQUIRE) That's floored me.   Any suggestions?

SQUIRE: All the better to see you with.

LUPE: All the better to see you with, my dear.

R. R. H.:   And, Granny, what big ears you've got.

LUPE: (to SQUIRE) how about that one?

SQUIRE: All the better to hear you with.

LUPE: (aside) Bit monotonous, isn't it? Still - (To her.) All the better to hear you with, my dear.

R. R. H.:   And, Granny, what big teeth you've got.

SQUIRE: (eagerly) All the better -

LUPE: (aside) All right, all right, I can guess, but I was hoping she wouldn't say that. (To her.) All the better to eat you with! (Leaps out of bed at her, but trips over his nightie. RED RIDING HOOD screams and turns to run.) Oh, blow this thing. (He rises pulling up the nightdress skirt and gives chase. They circle stage clockwise once and just as LUPE is coming towards door L the second time PRINCE bursts through it, brandishing axe. LUPE immediately flops to floor in a cowering bundle with hands over his neck.)

PRINCE: Red Riding Hood!)
) - (Together.)
R. R. H.:   Florizel!   )

SQUIRE:　　　　(popping head out L. of bed momentarily)　Curses! Foiled again!

(CHORUS pour on L.　SQUIRE gets out from under bed and creeps behind them to door L.)

CHORUS:　　　　Red Riding Hood!　Red Riding Hood!

PRINCE:　　　　It's all right, she's safe.　But I'll make sure it can never happen again.　(Raises axe.)

LUPE:　　　　No! Spare me! Spare me! I'll talk! It wasn't my idea. He made me do it - him! Him, under the bed there!

(General reaction.　1ST CHORUS looks under bed.)

1ST CHORUS:　　There's nobody here.

LUPE:　　　　Yes, there is, the Squire! The Squire!

2ND CHORUS:　　No, there's the Squire.

(SQUIRE stops guiltily in doorway.)

LUPE:　　　　See, he was sneaking out.

SQUIRE:　　　　Nonsense, I was sneaking in.　I mean, I was coming in - yes, coming in to save me pretty little distant cousin from your fiendish fangs.

(HARDY and FOOLHARDY run on L.)

H & F :　　　　Papa! Papa!

HARDY:　　　　We lost her, papa, Dame Trot.

(SQUIRE tries to shush them.)

FOOLHARDY:　　Yes, you know you told us to dump her in the Forest so that the wolf could get in here to -

SQUIRE:　　　　BELT UP!

PRINCE:　　　　(turning to SQUIRE)　So, it was you.

R. R. H. :　　　Granny! Where is granny? Don't say the wolf got her?

(There is a thump at the door R. and it shudders.)

What's that?

(All turn to look.   Another thump and shudder.)

PRINCE: Open it, somebody, open it!

(3RD CHORUS opens it.   DAME hurtles through, head down, tied to a kitchen chair and gagged and lands on bed.)

R. R. H. :   Granny!   )
) - (Together.)
OTHERS: Dame Trot!   )

R. R. H. :   Granny, what happened?   Are you all right?

(DAME tries to talk through gag.)

PRINCE: Untie her!

(CHORUS quickly release her from chair and untie gag.)

R. R. H. :   There, granny, what happened to you?

DAME: (indignantly) What happened?   What happened?   I'll tell you what happened - (Takes large breath to do so then stops.   Mildly.) There now, isn't that silly, I've quite forgotten.

PRINCE: I think I can guess, and it's all his doing.

SQUIRE: (going on knees) Forgive me! Forgive me! I only did it for the money.

DAME: Yes, go on, dear, forgive him, because - (Shyly whispers in RED RIDING HOOD'S ear.)

R. R. H. :   Well, of course I'll forgive him for you, granny.

(DAME crosses to stand in front of the still kneeling SQUIRE.)

DAME: Oh, Squire, this is so sudden.   But yes.

SQUIRE: Eh?   (Rising and moving away, horrified.)   Oh, no!

DAME: (pulling him back firmly) Oh, yes!

(Others laugh.)

PRINCE: What shall I do about this fellow?

LUPE: Spare me! Spare me!

(BAA and BAA-BAA run on L. and go affectionately to LUPE.)

Oh no! (Offering neck.) Don't spare me.

R. R. H.:   We'd better give him to Bo Peep to look after. Where is
Bo Peep, by the way?

PRINCE: And where's Poppet, come to that? We all started out
together. Never mind, there's one other very important matter to be
settled, Red Riding Hood. I know I'm only a humble woodcutter, but
it's just because that's all I am I can ask you this. Will you -

(BO PEEP and POPPET run on at R. back of Auditorium and down a
catwalk.)

POPPET: Your highness! Prince Florizel!

ALL: What?

POPPET: Come on, Bo Peep, this way, we're right at last.

PRINCE: Oh no, Poppet. For once you're quite, quite wrong.

POPPET: But your highness.

R. R. H.:   Why does he keep calling you "your highness"?

BO PEEP: Well, you see, he is. He's the real Prince.

(General reaction.)

R. R. H.:   And because of that you can't ask me - what you were going
to ask me?

(PRINCE tries to answer her and shakes head miserably.)

POPPET: Of course you can, sir. Try, sir, try! It's easy - look.
Bo Peep, will you marry me?

BO PEEP: Yes.

POPPET: Thanks. You see, easy! As easy as falling off a log.
That's it - woodcutters - remember!

PRINCE: (quietly) No, that's no good any more, Poppet. I'm a
Prince again and - and (Shakes head and turns to go.)

(WHITE FLASH R and enter FAIRY R.)

FAIRY: And I shall end this irksome curse.
You'll think my sense of time gets worse,
But there's two babes I had to save.
But now - henceforth, sweet Prince, be brave
And fear no more a lady's glance.

(Waves wand over him.   MUSIC ting.)

That's done and though you'll look at me askance
I have at once to whisk south east
And deal with Beauty and her Beast.

(Exit FAIRY R.)

PRINCE: Poppet, you're quite right.   It is as easy as falling off a
log.   Red Riding Hood, will you marry me?

R. R. H. : We-ll -

BO PEEP: Oh, go on, Red Riding Hood, it's just as easy to say yes.

R. R. H. : I know, but I wanted to make it last.   (To PRINCE.) Yes,
- woodcutter.

PRINCE: Thank you - Princess.

ALL: Hurrah!   *theres a kind 1 hush.*

MUSIC 52.   "WHAT A LOVELY EVENING"

Oh what a lovely evening
When your heart-beat quickens
As the plot unthickens.
Oh what a lovely evening
With a happy fusion
The foregone conclusion.
In this little tale of fun and laughter
Everyone lives happy ever after.
Oh what a lovely evening
When you're young and healthy, happy and in love.

BLACKOUT

(Close traverse tabs.)

ACT TWO

SCENE ELEVEN - WOLF CUBS

(LUPE runs on L. and SQUIRE R.   Both are looking over their shoulders and collide in C.)

BOTH: Why don't you - Oh, it's you.   (They rise.)

SQUIRE: Where are you off to in such a hurry?

LUPE: I'm running away.   I'm a failure as a wolf.   They're threatening to make me a shepherd.

SQUIRE: I'm running away, too.   I'm a failure as a villain.   Dame Trot's threatening to make me into a respectable married man.

BOTH: It's not fair.

LUPE: And you know whose fault it is -

(Enter a very miserable DEMON L in a pixie hood.

BOTH: His!

DEMON: No, pleath, don't get at me, I pray.
                 They have demoted me today.
                 Not e'en to imp or elf, alath!
                 But down to pixie, thecond clath.

(Enter FAIRY R, with an even more highly ornamented pair of lorgnettes.)

FAIRY: Well, here we have a sorry crew.

LUPE &
SQUIRE: It's all her fault.

DEMON: Yeth.   Go and thtew.

FAIRY: How very rude, but never mind,
                 I shall not harbour thoughts unkind.
                 To tell the truth, I'm rather pleas'd,
                 My future tasks will all be eas'd
                 For I have won a special prize -
                 New Magic lorgnettes for my eyes!

(Shows them.)

They can both past and future show,
For they're bifocal ones you know.

(Putting them to eyes.)

And what is this that I can see?
I've been appointed Fairy G.,
To three new wards.   I wonder who?

(A parchment descends from flies.   MUSIC whizz.)

Ah, the official posting's through.

(Reads.)

"Lupe the Wolf, False Hood the Knight,
And Pixie second class, Sheerspite."

ALL 3:   Oh no!

FAIRY: Oh yes.

(Fly parchment.)

DEMON: Well, I could thpit.

FAIRY: You did.

(DEMON stamps with frustrated rage.)

                But just the teeniest bit.
Come, come, don't sulk like little boys.
If evil now has lost its joys,
Then try instead to do some good.

DEMON: Thome good!

SQUIRE: Some good!

LUPE: Yes, p'raps we should.

SQUIRE: Let's try it.

DEMON: All right.

FAIRY: That's the way!
Just start with one good deed a day.

SQUIRE: You mean like Wolf Cubs do?   What fun!

LUPE: We never did when I was one.

FAIRY: (to SQUIRE)
                Well, let me pat you on the back!

        (Does so.)

                The very thing - a Wolf Cub pack!

        (Claps hands and four Wolf Cub caps are handed on to her.   Gives them
        out.)

                I shall, of course, Cub mistress be,
                And lead you on a goodness spree!

        MUSIC 53.   "WOLF CUBS".

ALL: We're the Wolf Cubs of old England,
                And England's in our care.
                If ever there is trouble about
                The Wolf Cubs will be there.

SQUIRE: I want to get my Collector's Badge
                To work for which I'm willing,
                When we go for a Bob-a-Job
                I'm the one to collect the shilling!

ALL: We're the Wolf Cubs etc.

LUPE: I want to get my Cookery Badge;
                A real good cook am I.
                When prime lamb chops aren't in the shops
                I can still make People Pie!

ALL: We're the Wolf Cubs etc.

DEMON: I want to get my Thplither'th Badge
                With help from dear Dame Trot.
                Will Granny help me tie a reef,
                Or elth will Granny-knot?

ALL: We're the Wolf Cubs etc.

FAIRY: I want the finest Wolf Cub pack;
                Their standard will be splendid;
                And I will accept the Cub salute
                In the way it was intended.

ALL: We're the Wolf Cubs etc.

        (Exit L. and R.   MUSIC 54.   Traverse tabs open for Scene twelve.)

ACT TWO

SCENE TWELVE - THE GRAND WEDDING RECEPTION

(Full set, Palace scene.

CHORUS enter L. and R. on rostrum two by two.   They meet in C. of rostrum, come down steps to D. C, bow and split, backing away, to form diagonal lines L. and R.   Principals follow similar procedure and form diagonal lines in front of CHORUS.   DEMON from L. on rostrum and FAIRY from R, backing to L. and R: BAA from L. and BAA-BAA from R, both backing to R: HARDY from L. and FOOLHARDY from R, both backing to L: BO PEEP from R, backing to R: SQUIRE from L, backing to L: POPPET from R, backing to R: LUPE from L, backing to L: DAME TROT from R, backing to R.   MUSIC 55. Fanfare.   All turn in.   PRINCE enters R. on rostrum, RED RIDING HOOD L, and meet in C.)

ALL: Hurrah!

(PRINCE and RED RIDING HOOD move down to take their bow. Principals move down into straight line with them.   CHORUS move up onto rostrum.)

PRINCE: Now all's turn'd out just as it should,
              For I have won Red Riding Hood.

R. R. H. :   And I dear Prince Florizel;
              So now our tale's no more to tell.

DAME: And very nicely spoken, too.
              But I've one thing to say to you
              Before you go to take your ease,
              And that is - oh -

ALL: REMINDER, PLEASE!

(AUDIENCE shout.)

DAME: No, no! It's come to me all right -
              'Twas Happy New Year and -

ALL: ● Goodnight.

MUSIC 56. "FINALE".

              Now our girl and boy have full employment
              We hope you have shared in our enjoyment.

Oh, what a lovely evening
To be playing, playing in a Pantomime.

CURTAIN

FURNITURE AND PROPERTY PLOT

ACT ONE

Set throughout play:

Little flower bed in front of R.
prosc. arch concealing forget-
me-not plant and a note on
either side.

ACT ONE Scene One

Set:

Two hay sheaves by farmhouse wing, L.
Large wooden rake R.

Off L:

Crook (BO-PEEP)
Very small suitcase with Royal Crest (POPPET)
Very large suitcase (POPPET)

In it:

    Small portable chair
    Small red carpet
    Portable gramophone
    Bedding roll
    Board with switch
    Two prop axes

Very long haired wig (HARDY)

Off R:

Pair of coconut shells (SQUIRE)
Twosome two-way scooter with wheels
and handle-bars at each end (HARDY & FOOLHARDY)
Letter with large red seal (HARDY)
Large pair of glasses (FOOLHARDY)
Car steering wheel fitted onto a crossbar
holding two practical car head lamps and hooter (DAME TROT)
Shopping basket with red cloak (DAME TROT)
Large bottle labelled "SILVIKRIN" (SQUIRE)

Personal:

SQUIRE: Riding crop with safety pin on end

2.

Off R:

    Card (DEMON's fixture list)   (FAIRY)

To descend from flies or Off L:

    Hair restorer bottle (DEMON)

Personal:

    FAIRY: Wand,
              Ornamental lorgnettes
              Pendant watch

ACT ONE Scene Three

Set:

In front of Wolf's door U. C:

    Green mat with key underneath it
    Log L. C.

Off Wolf's Lair U. C:

    Duster, little apron, broom
    Two sheets prepared for tearing
    Cook's hat and butcher's apron
    Mincing machine
    Small sheepskin
    Small fishing rod and bottle, labelled "MINT SAUCE"

Off R:

    Check Poppet's axe
    Large steak (FAIRY)

Off L:

    Check Prince's axe

ACT ONE Scene Four

Set:

    In blackout, old sign post pointing L to
    "HOOD HALL" with 2 hooks on it

Off R:

    Two pairs handcuffs (LUPE)
    Check Poppet's and Prince's axe

3.

ACT ONE Scene Five

Set:

Will in fireplace
Note in fireplace
Note under stairs
Loose stone marked with an "X" in pillar
Note behind loose stone

Off L:

Tomato, flower pot and balloon painted to
represent marrow

Off R:

Two ghost sheets (HARDY and FOOLHARDY)
Rope to tie round Lupe
Ghost sheet (POPPET)
Two ghost table cloths (BO-PEEP and RED RIDING HOOD)
Handbag (DAME)
Check Prince's axe
Check pin on Squire's riding crop

ACT TWO Scene Six

Set:

Counter diagonally R.

On it:

Some papers
Wig block with wig
Large book entitled "EXERCISES"
Bowl marked "FINEST SQUELCHY MUD" (made from
calcium carbonate and chocolate)

Below counter:

Hat stand

Hairdresser's chair with waterproof sheet U. L

R. of hairdresser's chair

Trolley

On it:

Bathcap, tumbler, towel,
Three over-sized tins of pancake make-up,
"Autumn Leaf Tan", "Peach Bloom Blush" and "Rose Petal Pink"

4.

<u>Set</u>: (Cont'd.)

        Wig on wig block
        Hand mirror
        Headscarf
        Bowl of mud pack
        Watering can

<u>L. of hairdresser's chair</u>:

    Trolley

    <u>On it</u>:

        Milk filled rubber glove
        Prop hair dryer with switch and rubber tubing
          to stirrup pump
        Over-sized tin Cherry Blossom black polish
        Bowl of mud pack
        Tin labelled "DRIED MILK"
        Jug of water

<u>Off R</u>:

    Will (DAME)
    Handbag (DAME)
    Permanent waving machine to descend from flies fitted with a number
    of dangling clips to look like a large spider

ACT TWO Scene Eight

<u>Set</u>:

    Bench U. R. C in front of rostrum

<u>Off L</u>:

    Paper similar to will (HARDY)
    Flunky's staff (PRINCE)
    Two leashes (BAA and BAA-BAA)
    Goblet (SQUIRE)
    Two small gilt chairs (HARDY)
    Small table (FOOLHARDY)
    Huge bottle labelled "M. FINN'S ORIGINAL
      KNOCK-OUT DROPS" (HARDY & FOOLHARDY)
    Wine cup bowl (DEMON)
    Basket of goodies (FOOLHARDY)

ACT TWO Scene Nine

Off L:

      Stretcher (HARDY & FOOLHARDY)
      Check basket of goodies (RED RIDING HOOD)

Off R:

      Little bank with cluster of woodland flowers and plant
      with dock leaves, attached to a thin batten of wood which
      goes underneath the frontcloth so the plant can be made
      to slide along from behind cloth, to be set in blackout

Set at back of Auditorium:

      Cup of coffee (FAIRY)

ACT TWO Scene Ten

Set:

In front of window L:

      Small table

      On it:

          Pot plant
          Shopping basket

      Bed R. C.

      Over it:

          Cover and red cloak at foot

      In it:

          Warming pan

          Club under pillow

L. of bed:

      Chair with nightdress and mob cap

R. of bed:

      Table

      On it:

          Candlestick
          Prop bending candle

Off L:

        Basket of goodies (RED RIDING HOOD)
        Axe (PRINCE)

Off R:

        Cup and saucer (DAME)
        Kitchen chair with robe and gag (DAME)

ACT TWO Scene Eleven

Parchment to descend from flies R.

Off R:

        Four wolf cub caps

1.   Forget-Me-Not Plant

This can have detachable edible leaves, made of dyed rice paper. The flower bed can be set in front of L pros. arch if it can be more conveniently worked there. The plant is worked by a thin line running through a screw-eye or over a pulley to behind pros. arch by which it can be pulled up. The flower bed should be of a sufficient height to conceal the various leaves, being attached. Seven leaves are used altogether.

2.   Candle in Scene Ten

The kind of flexible tubing used for some desk lamps is suitable for this Two lines attached to candlestick, one on R. side going off R. to pull it R. The other on L. side of candlestick, threaded through a screw-eye at L. end of table and then going off R. to pull it L. Nylon or fishing line should be used.

MUSIC PLOT

PART 1

1. Overture.

Scene One.

2.	Opening Chorus, "WHAT A LOVELY MORNING"	Chorus.
3.	Bo Peep entrance music.	Orch.
4.	Red Riding Hood entrance music.	"
5.	"BEFORE I GROW TOO OLD"	Red Riding Hood and Chorus.
6.	Squire's entrance music.	Orch.
7.	Hardy and Foolhardy's entrance music	"
8.	Poppet's entrance music.	"
9.	Prince's entrance music.	"
10.	"SHOCKINGLY SHY"	Prince.
11.	Dame's entrance music.	Orch.
12.	"TUM TI TUM"	Dame.
13.	"HAPPY RETURNS"	Prince and Red Riding Hood.
14.	Sheep's entrance music.	Orch.
15.	"GET TO KNOW YOU BETTER"	Poppet and Bo Peep.
16.	"WHAT A LOVELY MORNING", reprise 2. (Continue, orchestra only, as link to next scene.)	Ensemble.

Scene Two.

17.	Fairy music.	Orch.
18.	Demon Music.	"
19.	"BE BAD" (Continue, orchestra only, as link to next scene.)	Squire and Demon.

Scene Three.

20.	Wolf music.	Orch.
21.	"I LIKE PEOPLE"	Lupe.
22.	"ISN'T IT SURPRISING?"	Prince and Poppet.
23.	Fairy music, reprise 17.	Orch.
24.	Shimmering music.	"
25.	Sheep music, reprise 14.	"
26.	" " "	"
27.	"LITTLE BO PEEP" (Continue, orchestra only, as link to next scene.)	Ensemble.

Scene Four.

| 28. | Hardy and Foolhardy music, reprise 7. | Orch. |
| 29. | "NOTHING UPSTAIRS"
(Continue, orchestra only, as link to
next scene.) | Hardy and Foolhardy. |

Scene Five.

30.	Mysterioso music.	Orch.
31.	Sheep music, reprise 14.	"
32.	Composite cue, including Ballet and Scene Finale.	Fairy, Demon and Chorus.

PART II

| 33. | Entr'acte. |

Scene Six.

| 34. | "BEAUTY-FULL!" | Ensemble. |
| 35. | Production number.
(Continue, orchestra only, as link to
next scene.) | " |

Scene Seven.

36.	Sheep music, reprise 14.	Orch.
37.	"BAA-BAA-BAA" (Continue, orchestra only, as link to next scene.)	Dame, Sheep and Audience.

Scene Eight.

38.	"WALLFLOWERS"	Bo Peep and Chorus.
39.	Sheep music, reprise 14, (very fast tempo.)	Orch.
40.	"SOMEBODY"	Prince and Red Riding Hood.
41.	Demon and luring music.	Orch.
42.	"DANCING TIME"	Squire, Dame, Hardy and Foolhardy.
43.	"WALLFLOWERS", reprise 38.	Orch.
44.	" " " (Continue as link to next scene.)	"

Scene Nine.

45.	Hardy and Foolhardy music, reprise 7.	Orch.
46.	Demon's spell.	"
47.	Fairy music, reprise 17.	"
48.	Shimmering music, reprise 24.	"
49.	Demon music, reprise 18. (Continue as line to next scene.)	"

Scene Ten.

50.	"WHEN I WAS YOUNG"	Dame.
51.	Wolf music, reprise 20.	Orch.
52.	"WHAT A LOVELY EVENING", reprise 2. (Continue, orchestra only, as link to next scene.)	Ensemble.

Scene Eleven.

      53.   "WOLF CUBS"   Squire, Lupe,
                                                Demon and Fairy.

      54.   "WHAT A LOVELY MORNING", reprise Orch.
           2 as link to next scene and continue
           as music for walk-down.   Orch.

Scene Twelve.

      55.   Fanfare.   Orch.

      56.   "FINALE", reprise 2.   Tutti.